D1316390

June 20, 1996

Dear Clifton,

I continue to grow up with you as I read your compelling coming-of-age memoirs, and I am grateful for the experience.

In your first book, *When We Were Colored*, I met the remarkable community that treasured your life, and I found myself seated beside you on Southern steps, sharing your dream of going north. In your second book, I traveled with you on *The Last Train North* and experienced your disappointment when St. Louis, the city of your dreams, proved not to be the mecca of equality and opportunity that you had been led to expect. I also shared in that book your early encounters with the Civil Rights movement and your fear of being shipped off to Vietnam when you became a soldier.

Now, in *Watching Our Crops Come In*, I find myself standing with you near the banks of the Potomac, when, as a young airman assigned to the 89th Presidential Wing, you could only watch as the 1960s brought sweeping changes to your Mississippi Delta world, and indeed to the entire country. Through the honesty and simplicity of your writing, I can also feel the mixture of personal anxiety and hope that filled your days as you were forced to stand on the sidelines of that great struggle in our country's life—a struggle that remains unfinished today.

Thank you, Clifton, for inviting me and all of your other readers to share the journey of your life, a distinctly hopeful American life that keeps faith with your elders, who never stopped dreaming of a more just and compassionate world. I share your hope and their dream.

Your friend,

Robert F. Kennedy, Jr.

Watching Our
Crops Come In

Also by Clifton Taulbert

When We Were Colored
The Last Train North

CERTIFICATE OF

Promotion

THIS IS TO CERTIFY _Clifton Lemuel Taulbert_

has satisfactorily completed the Course of Study as prescribed

for the _9th Grade_ _of the_ _Moore Elementary_

and is therefore entitled to this testimonial and to

admission to the _9th Grade_

Given at _Glen Allan, Mississippi_ _this_

Principal

Watching Our
Crops Come In

Clifton L. Taulbert

Viking

VIKING
Published by the Penguin Group
Penguin Books USA Inc., 375 Hudson Street,
New York, New York 10014, U.S.A.
Penguin Books Ltd, 27 Wrights Lane,
London W8 5TZ, England
Penguin Books Australia Ltd, Ringwood,
Victoria, Australia
Penguin Books Canada Ltd, 10 Alcorn Avenue,
Toronto, Ontario, Canada M4V 3B2
Penguin Books (N.Z.) Ltd, 182–190 Wairau Road,
Auckland 10, New Zealand

Penguin Books Ltd, Registered Offices:
Harmondsworth, Middlesex, England

First published in 1997 by Viking Penguin,
a division of Penguin Books USA Inc.

1   3   5   7   9   10   8   6   4   2

Photographs from the author's collection and
from the National Archives.

LIBRARY OF CONGRESS CATALOGING IN PUBLICATION DATA
Taulbert, Clifton L.
Watching our crops come in / Clifton L. Taulbert.
p.   cm.
ISBN 0-670-85952-4
1. Taulbert, Clifton L.   2. Afro-Americans—Washington (D.C.)—
Biography.   3. United States. Air Force—Afro-Americans—
Biography.   4. Civil rights movements—United States—
History—20th century.   5. Afro-Americans—Civil rights.
6. Vietnamese Conflict, 1961–1975—United States.
7. United States—History—1961–1969.
I. Title.
F205.N4T38   1997
973.923'092—dc20
[B]   96-31230

This book is printed on acid-free paper.

∞

Printed in the United States of America
Set in Weiss   Designed by Virginia Norey

43074 - Ingram 3/97

dedicated

... to the memory of my soldier friends, whose courage outgrew their fear as they left me behind and set out to fight a war they barely understood in the Mekong Delta, so far from the delta in Mississippi that I called home.

... to the foot soldiers of the civil rights movement, the ordinary people from all walks of life who without training or commission voluntarily joined a cause on my behalf because of their vision of how a true democracy should look, feel, and behave.

... to my mother, Mary Morgan Taulbert, who saw her sights lifted with the tide of the movement, dropped her maid's apron, and donned her teaching mantle, pouring her life into the children she taught and the teachers she administered in a little project called Head Start.

... to my sister Clara Taulbert White, and my cousin Dr. Joyce O. Jenkins, who bravely left our small town of Glen Allan for the hallowed halls at "Ole Miss" to enroll, to study, to be jailed, and to excel, becoming part of the crops harvested during the season of the civil rights era.

Contents

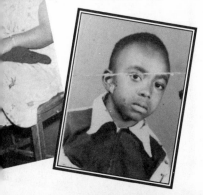

INTRODUCTION

In 1963, *I left my home* in Glen Allan, Mississippi, and headed north with plans to do well and make my family proud. Nurtured by the voices of the family and friends who had reared me and believed in me, I was determined to get a good job, go to college, and return each summer to the house where I had been born. Instead, the train took me to the reality of northern life, my first taste of the civil rights movement, and the prospect of being drafted into the army and shipped to Vietnam. By 1966, I had joined the United States Air Force, I had been classified, and I was becoming a man.

Many of my friends were shipped to a delta far away—one strikingly different from the Mississippi Delta where I grew up. As I watched and waited for my own Vietnam orders, which mercifully never came, the once tranquil South I had known as a child was issuing orders to a new breed of soldiers. These "soldiers" were making front-page news as the civil rights movement penetrated the cotton communities that I had left behind. But as the war dragged on in Southeast Asia and ordinary citizens were enlisting in the movement back home, I stood, as it were, on the "turn-roads"—not real roads at all but spaces in the fields where farmers turn their tractors and children play—and watched from a distance as my world changed.

Saved by a special assignment from being sent to Vietnam and prohibited by my uniform from joining the fight for freedom back home, I grew up on the turn-roads, watching the crops come in. This is the story of those years and the harvest that I saw.

Watching Our
Crops Come In

HAMPTON PLANTATION

Purchased in 1840's by Hampton family. In fifties, sixties & seventies operated by and at intervals was residence of Wade Hampton III, distinguished CSA General & first governor of S.C. after Reconstruction.

SCHOOL DAYS 1952-53
GLEN ALLEN

Outstanding Achievement

For WING SUPPLY "PRIDE" MAN OF THE MONTH

to A2C CLIFTON L. TAULBERT   AF17697936

397th Supply Squadron - Dow Air Force Base, Maine

for Outstanding performance of duty as the 75th Fighter Interceptor Squadron Supply Point Monitor for Base Supply. For willingness to assume increased responsibility and ability to accomplish any task related to your career field. For continuing pursuit of higher education.

from 1 March 1966   **to** 31 March 1966

MARVIN G. WALKER, LT COL, USAF
COMMANDER

JOHN E. BOOTH, MAJOR, USAF
BASE SUPPLY OFFICER

ONE

Bright Boy
from the Delta

It *was winter,* 1967, early in the year. Like thousands of other soldiers, I had lived for months with the fear that I would one day receive orders that would carry me far from home, into the random terrors of the war in Vietnam, which we witnessed daily on TV. None of this had been my plan. In August of 1964, to circumvent the draft, I had joined the air force. After basic training at Lackland Air Force Base and technical school in Amarillo, Texas, I was assigned to Dow Air Force Base in Bangor, Maine, a place I had barely heard of and knew little about. By now, I had seen two hard northeastern winters and I wanted to see no more. But I wanted Vietnam even less.

However, on this midwinter day, I could hardly believe my good fortune. Standing outside the post office in the cold, bright air, I read again and again a letter that informed me that I had been selected to serve in a classified position at Andrews Air Force Base in Washington, D.C. "Congratulations," it said. Congratulations! All I could see was that word. I had survived an extensive background check, and now I could tell my great news to everyone except my best friend, Paul Demuniz, who had already shipped out for Vietnam. I was sad for Paul, but elated for myself. This was not a pipe dream. It was a real assignment, one that would make any airman proud. But it wasn't "any airman," it was me, Cliff, the little boy who had grown up in the village of Glen Allan, in the Mississippi Delta, living first with Poppa, my great-grandfather, and later with Ma Ponk, my great-aunt, under whose stern but loving eye I spent my high school years.

It was a long walk but a good one back to the barracks from the post office. As I moved along the quiet path, alone except for an occasional passing car, I recalled how badly as a child I had wanted to go north and how much I hated picking and chopping cotton. But as long as I was in Ma Ponk's care, I knew I had to work and be ready every morning to catch Mr. Walter's truck, which never broke down, no matter how much I prayed.

With the letter of my good news safely put away in my

satchel, I walked and whistled as I thought about Ma Ponk and my childhood dreaming. "Boy, git off them steps, wash yore hands, and git back here to dis kitchen," I could still hear her yelling from the back of her small frame house. "You know we got to git up early to catch that darn field truck."

Thus she would catch me resting on the front porch steps, still wet from the day's sweat but enjoying any breeze the evening swept my way, and I would hurry back to the kitchen so that I could eat, get the chickens in, and get ready for bed. Some nights, the sun would leave a trail of colors as it moved across the sky and would look as if it was going to fall right on top of our neighbor Miss Elsie's house. I dreamed of the day that I'd no longer have to eat fast, go to bed early, and get up before the roosters. I dreamed of going north, where there were no cotton fields, just good jobs.

Good jobs, I thought, as I walked up the small paved sidewalk to my barracks. I wanted to run into the building shouting the news of my good job, but instead I entered the back door by the fire escape, the one that was hardly used except as our weekend gathering place. Weekdays, our barracks were tense with the fear of impending orders. Most of the guys just went about their routine, watching the news, reading the bulletin board, and waiting for the weekend to arrive, when the mental war we waged could be put on hold. Since this was not the weekend, I hesitated to blurt out my news. I just walked up the inside stairs to the second floor and quietly approached the room that I shared with Airman Robuck from New Jersey.

Robuck was fearful of the war, but he had managed to adopt a "so what" attitude. If he had to go, I expected he would go and do what he was supposed to do. I wanted to talk to Robuck, but I hoped now to find the room empty. I needed time to reflect on this new assignment and what it could mean. In our hall, one guy stood talking on a pay phone, but everything else was quiet. I nodded at him as I got out my key to unlock my door.

When I opened the door, only the heavy smell of furniture oil and wax greeted me. Robuck wasn't back from work. I sat down in the green vinyl chair that was equally spaced between the single bed and the bunk beds, pulled the letter out of my satchel, and looked at it again. Only a few of my close friends knew how fearful I had been about the prospect of Vietnam. We seldom discussed fear, perhaps because refraining from such discussions seemed to be part of the rite of becoming a man. I just knew that I wanted to live to become a man, and I kept quiet when members of the group loudly discussed how they would handle a deadly situation. I would watch in silence as they pretended to crouch in foxholes, crawl through jungle brush, or wade through rice paddies with their imaginary weapons held high above their heads. Even though I was part of them, I never felt as "ready" for battle as they appeared to be. And I never felt I had the character and skills required to be the kind of soldier who could kill so as not to be killed. Fear had caused me to enlist to escape the draft, and I surprised myself when I not only made it through basic training but also made it with honors. However, once in, I still lived with the prospect of my being reassigned to a remote supply post in Southeast Asia. Now that prospect had itself become remote with this new assignment—an assignment I almost hadn't applied for.

Like the rest of the guys, I daily watched the bulletin board, praying not to see my name. I never dreamed that I would find there a notice that would save my life. The bulletin board was always surrounded at the end of the day, and Orell Clay, an airman from New York, was always there, his body blocking our view. Since he was big and mouthy, I felt it best to give him room, although some of the guys would elbow him aside. On the day I found my notice, I waited while Orell and Fred Crowly, his white roommate from Rhode Island, looked at every piece of posted information. When at last they left, I moved to the spot they had vacated and was relieved to see that there was no word of any need for additional troops in Vietnam. Just as I was about to walk away and join my friends at the mess hall, a small bulletin from Strategic Air Command (SAC) headquarters in Nebraska caught my eye. A new slot, a classified position, had opened at Andrews Air Force Base in Washington, D.C. Reading more closely, I realized that the job description fell under my air force classification. AF 17697936 was administrative supply, and they needed someone with my skills. For a brief moment, I fantasized that I could win this post, but I was also sure that I had no chance. Although the military was more integrated than anyplace I had ever seen, I somehow felt that this job would go to a white airman. I didn't want to apply only to be disappointed, but I wrote down the information anyway, and tucked it in my pocket as I walked from the barracks to the mess hall.

That night, I reconsidered. Maybe I did have a chance. After all, back home in Glen Allan I had applied and had been hired for a job in Mr. Hilton's grocery store that had historically been reserved for white boys. Believing that just maybe I could do it again, I completed the form requested and mailed it in. I told no one, not even my closest friends. I then planned to forget the exercise. I knew that thousands of airmen just like me would have read the same announcement and would be thinking, as I was, that this assignment could limit their chances of being shipped off to Vietnam. I returned to my routine of shipping aircraft parts from base to base and to my continuing fear of Vietnam. Days stretched into weeks, and weeks into months, and Dow Air Force Base was beginning to feel more like home than I wanted.

Home for me would always be Glen Allan, and it felt strange to find myself becoming comfortable in a place where the snow fell as frequently as rain. The Mississippi

Delta was my home, and I wanted to live so that I could return to the house built by my great-grandfather Sidney Peter. Grandpa had come from Demopolis, Alabama, to the Delta, where he encountered other "colored" who had migrated from Natchez, from Louisiana, and from as far away as South Carolina. Only one generation removed from slavery, these people had held on to their dreams and had built their homes to give place to them. The front porches became the place where visiting relatives from up north would sit and spin their intoxicating tales of northern life. And as long as I can remember, the tales were told each summer. And I remembered them all.

Legal segregation kept the wonderful older people, on whose porches we sat, from using official meeting places such as the library and the community room at the town's clinic, but they seemed not to have cared. Their front porches became their centers of command, from which they welcomed us into a world and a life that had barely changed since the early days of Jim Crow, the system that evolved once slavery stopped.

Like many small towns throughout the south, ours was a cotton community whose social order set the course for both white and colored babies. Miss Lottie, the town's colored midwife, brought me into the world, a world that had already relegated me to an inferior position, but one that could not negate the welcome I felt as a child growing up in the big house with the long front porch. During my years in this rambling wooden house infused with hopes, I started school and began my youthful dreaming.

Glen Allan was a safe place to dream. Although we lived day to day with the harshness of the Jim Crow laws and the limitations imposed by legal segregation, the elders in our community still managed to instill in us the will to live, work hard, and study long because they believed that tomorrow was always the brightest day. They understood the necessity to leave home and do well, but they expected you to return. This safe, predictable world would one day pass into history. But as I grew, I had the benefit of three generations of wisdom, wisdom that years later would serve me well as I was finding my own way.

As I approached my seventeenth birthday in 1963, I found myself preparing to leave for my first train ride and my journey north. St. Louis was my destination. I would live there, get a job, go to school, and return home to Glen Allan every summer, just as my idols, Uncle William Henry and Aunt Dora, from Chicago, and other relatives had done before me. It was a grand plan: the train ride north, the colored porter, and the bright city lights and paved streets. But it was not to be. Immersed in my own dreaming, I hadn't paid close attention to the outside world and the changes taking place. At home in the Delta, I was insulated by fields of cotton and by those who picked it, by lakes of brim and catfish and those who caught them. No one had pulled me aside to tell me about the civil rights movement or the other delta, so far away in

Vietnam. They left me to my chopping and picking cotton and dreaming on my own. Little did I know that the fantasy world up north I had created in my mind while working Miss Jefferson's fields would one day be derailed by the reality of war and a social revolution.

The unraveling began after I arrived in St. Louis, where I lived in a small room over a small store, in a city I had dreamed about but barely knew. Suddenly I found myself on my own, hundreds of miles away from the people who knew me best. Even though my natural father had paid for my ticket to St. Louis, I really did not know him. He had left the Delta as a young man, gone north, and created a new life for himself. I had been excited over the prospect of a relationship with him, but it never materialized as I had hoped. I don't question his joy in seeing me, but I soon learned that his life in St. Louis had little room for me. He had arranged for me to stay with relatives I had never met. For the first time in my life I found myself acting, thinking, and doing on my own.

At night, while sharing my small room with a younger cousin, I tried to sort out my feelings. Would I be able to find a good job? I had been led to believe that color was not a factor here, only skills, and I knew that I was skilled. After all, I had been given a white boy's job back home and had graduated as valedictorian of my small high school class. But the long-promised good life with the good job, where whites and blacks lived and worked together, was fraught with complexities that I hadn't understood. Still, I was determined to press forward in spite of all that wasn't there, to dig deep beneath that reality and to find a way to make my dreams come true.

For about a year, things went well enough. I was becoming a northerner. I had started school at the St. Louis branch of the American Institute of Banking and had almost lost my southern accent, a sure sign that I was becoming one of those who would one day return south to visit in the summer. However, as I moved toward social acculturation, the reality of a military conflict expanding into war invaded the world I knew. America was sending thousands of young men, mostly black, to Vietnam. I watched them leave St. Louis in the prime of their life, never to return. As the war wore on, I was sure that one day I would be drafted, too, and I was scared. Having just begun to live, I didn't want to die. But I was black, and it seemed as if black soldiers formed the ranks of the front line in Vietnam.

Although I had friends, I had no one to counsel me, not even my father, but I had grown up more than I realized as I faced the prospect of being drafted. In the quietness of my heart, a heart shaped in the Delta, I decided to enlist in the air force to escape an army draft and possible death in Vietnam. No one knew better than I that I was not gun-toting soldier material. Though handling guns was a way of life in the South, I couldn't shoot straight and had never killed, bagged, or skinned anything. In light of what I knew, the air force seemed like the best place for me. And it was. Again, I boarded a train, this time the Texas Lone

Star to San Antonio, where I started basic training. With a shaved head, five sets of white boxer shorts, and uniforms that didn't fit properly, I became an airman in August 1964.

Basic training was different. Unlike Glen Allan and even St. Louis, there were no nurturing front porches and caring people to hold my hand, just a stranger neatly dressed in a starched uniform and dark glasses, a drill sergeant who asked no questions and expected none. He only barked orders. However, with the help of such friends as Jerry Williams, James Rinderknect, and Airman Canty, I actually managed to adapt to the new and challenging world of "orders." We learned to march to them all. Too afraid to mess up, I did my best in basic training and even later became a junior barracks leader while in technical school in Amarillo, Texas. Still young and afraid, I was slowly becoming a soldier. Most of the men were as apprehensive as I was, although we all tried not to show it. We had started to learn that the military was there to make men out of us, not to deal with our idealistic views and youthful fears.

Amarillo was indeed a detour for me. I had dreamed only of going north to live, not of becoming a soldier in Texas, sitting in a barracks worrying about my orders. When my permanent orders came, I was relieved. My fate was not as bad as I had imagined. Some of the guys who seemed to have connections had found themselves with orders to Florida, but for Kenneth Cone, James Rinderknect, and me, it was the cold Northeast, a cause for sober thankfulness, if not for jubilation. We were going not to Vietnam but to Dow Air Force Base in Maine.

At first I dreaded the assignment, the remoteness of it and the chilling prospect that I could still be sent at any time to Vietnam. As the war continued and the numbers of dead and wounded increased, I began to accept that being cold and isolated was better than being warm and wounded. After making up my mind to give Dow my best shot, it wasn't long before I began to feel like the others, just doing my job, biding my time, and waiting for orders that I hoped would never come.

Sometime after I applied for the classified position, a letter came, telling me that I was among the ones selected for a background investigation. If it proved positive, I would be given orders for reassignment to Washington, D.C. I had never been investigated before and had no idea what it entailed. The letter contained a questionnaire. I was to provide information about the people I knew and the places I had lived. I carefully answered each question, wondering all the time if this was really happening to me. Maybe my porch people were right, and tomorrow was the brightest day. I didn't want to tell my friends until the investigation was complete and I had an official answer. My heart held a secret that I wanted to share, but I kept it close to me.

Without being specific, I asked Sgt. Brown, a seasoned

airman, to explain to me what a classified background investigation included. When he asked why, I held him off, but I was still able to get him to tell me what I needed to know. As he talked, I realized that investigators would go to both Glen Allan and St. Louis. What a stir this would be for Glen Allan. It was so small that all news traveled fast, and this type of news would travel even faster than most.

The investigators would get all the information needed and then some if they happened to run into Miss Doll, our lady who everyone agreed was "tetched" in the head. She always seemed to intercept strangers who came looking for information from the colored side of the town. I had written down the names of my mother, Mary Taulbert, my aunt, Elna Boose, and Rev. McBeth, the colored principal. But if Miss Doll saw a strange car driving slowly, she would walk right up as close as she could and lean in the window. "I'm Louise Morris, pleased to make your acquaintance. New in town, I s'pose." I dreaded to think what she might dream up to tell them in her odd, rambling way. In St. Louis, I had provided the names of Madison Brazier and Oscar Guyton Sr., in whose homes I had stayed during my short time there.

In Glen Allan, the investigators would hear the story of my birth and meet the people who had welcomed me into the world. They would see that I had been among the fortunate ones to have been born in a town where caring had long been a way of life. Despite all hardships, I grew up being loved and learning from those who loved me, people who took their leisure on front porches, where they entertained us, nurtured us, and spoke the secrets of their hearts.

The investigators would learn all of this and more. They would learn about my aptitude as a student, which led to my being named valedictorian of my class. They would learn about my hard work not only in the fields but also in the local hardware store, owned by Mr. Freid, who had me assist him with his yearly inventory, and later in Mr. Hilton's grocery store. And they would learn about the life dreams that brought me to St. Louis and the confectionery at 2629 North Spring Avenue, where Uncle Madison ruled and reigned.

Uncle Madison and Mr. Guyton would tell them about my life in St. Louis, how I took on extra responsibility in my work at the confectionery, and how Jefferson Bank hired me at a time when there were no blacks in meaningful positions. They would learn how the civil rights activists protested the bank's hiring practices and how, after many demonstrations by young black St. Louisians, I was the one who was hired. Both men were proud of that and shared the story as if it were their own.

Dow Air Force Base was a long way from either Glen Allan or St. Louis, but in those two places lived the people who would help determine my chances to get that classified assignment. And now all I had to do was wait.

After the last weeks of fall had faded and the new year had begun, the private wait was over. I held the official letter that said "Congratulations," and now I could tell my friends. I was going to Washington, D.C., to work in the Eighty-ninth Presidential Wing at Andrews Air Force Base. The people at SAC headquarters had called me a "bright boy," which I took to be a compliment. Of course it could also have been military code suggesting that I was a good risk for this new assignment because the investigation into my past had turned up no evidence of past activities that would have proven to be an embarrassment to the government. But I would never know if their meaning was different from what I took it to be. I had always been told by the old people back home that I had "mother wit," by which they meant the natural ability to make a path for myself, and an old preacher from the colony, the all-black settlement just south of Glen Allan, had once told Poppa that I was marked for good. Thus I assumed that in calling me a "bright boy" the background investigators had made a similar determination about me.

Delighted as I was, I now began to think about the challenges I would face as a new airman. I wanted the job, but because I hadn't thought I'd get it, I had paid very little attention to the skill requirements. I was now apprehensive about my technical ability to do the job. Still, no matter my feelings, I had my orders. They were expecting me at the Eighty-ninth.

While I embraced my new assignment, I also felt a bit of remorse knowing that I'd be leaving Dow. During my last few weeks, as I walked to and from my barracks, a fading green cinderblock two-story building, I fixed in my mind a picture I didn't want to forget. Amid the weekday quiet, I stood at the foot of the fire escape, our entry to the barracks. On weekends in good weather, that fire escape came to life. It was our gathering place, where we yelled at each other, cut hair, and forgot the war. Like the stoops of New York, the verandahs of New Orleans, and even the porches of the Mississippi Delta, it was a small reminder of home, where we were welcomed and visited with friends. There, dates were made and broken, cars were borrowed, and the war was put on hold. In warm weather, we dressed in jeans, cut-offs, and white tee-shirts, our dog tags the only reminders of our military life. As I stood there in the quiet, I pictured all my friends, those of different races and from vastly different social backgrounds, gathering, leaning over the railings, sitting on the steps with the end doors of the barracks propped open wide so that we could all hear the music, our voices mingling in the air like a well-cooked gumbo.

Even though most of us were thankful that we had not been sent to Vietnam, on nights when we sat on the fire escape, we also wished that we were somewhere else, preferably in a city. Getting a good assignment at a base that was close to a city with a great night life was the dream of all the airmen I had come to know, but for most of us, those bases and their cities would always be somewhere else. When the word of my new assignment got around, they were all delighted for me. I was lucky, they said. I had my orders, and they wished me well.

I had only a few weeks left, but for the most part I was gone. My room on the second floor of the barracks would soon house another guy. I hoped that he would appreciate how well I had kept his side. I had put so much wax on the floor that all my replacement would have to do was just hit it softly with a buffer and the barracks sergeant would be pleased. Although our world was focused on the war, we still had to polish those floors, tighten those green blankets, and spit shine everything that didn't move. Often I felt this was a waste of time, but I was assured that obedience to such orders was essential preparation for combat, where commands had to be followed without question if you wanted to stay alive.

Excitement and apprehension about my Washington assignment pulled me on. I had never been to the District of Columbia, but the media had brought Washington to me. I was a little fearful of going there, yet I wanted to experience all it had to offer a young man not long removed from the Delta, where life, it had seemed, would never change. Now, as I readied myself for my new life, I knew that the South was changing as well, as the civil rights movement penetrated ever more deeply the world behind the cotton curtains.

When the day to leave Dow came, I was packed and ready early. Since I didn't have a car, I asked John Palozzi to drive me to the airport. We had become good friends, sharing great conversations and good Italian food. John lived in a barracks close to mine. When he arrived, with a little help from my roommate, we got my duffel bag and suitcases down the hall and down the fire escape.

Although we arrived at the Bangor airport early, the waiting room was full. I knew some of the airmen, and I could tell by their faces and snatches of their conversations that they had not been as lucky as I had been. We didn't talk. There was little to say. During those days, airports were not always the places of pleasure travel that we wanted them to be; they took us to our duty, a duty that we knew could claim our lives. John waited with me until it was time to check in, and seemingly within minutes I found myself on board, buckled in, and flying into my future.

While sitting quietly in the plane, I found myself both looking out and looking back. Much had happened in my life since I left the Mississippi Delta. I was no longer the innocent, dreaming boy who loved his great-grandfather's 1949 Buick, frozen custard ice cream, and hot French bread. The reality of becoming a soldier was maturing me, and my fear of Vietnam made me value the life I had. While stationed at Dow, I had seen scores of airmen shipped off to a war they barely understood, to fight a people they hardly knew. We had been told that they were going to ensure democracy, even though it was not fully realized here at home. As a child, I hadn't had to worry about such issues as democracy denied, because Poppa and my family had protected me as long as they could, but now I was out and on my own.

As my plane approached Washington National Airport,

I could see the Potomac shining below. I also caught my first glimpses of monuments I had only read about or seen in pictures. It was as though they were moving up to greet me. The plane moved in closer, and people all around me exclaimed at the sight of the Pentagon and the Washington Monument. Fathers and mothers pointed out the sights to their children, and I eagerly listened and craned my neck to see what they were seeing. I really was in Washington, and I tried desperately to catch sight of the Lincoln Memorial and the reflecting pool, which, after Dr. King's historic 1963 march, had come to symbolize the freedom that my people cherished.

Years earlier, I had left Glen Allan, Mississippi, loaded with dreams, my family's, our friends', and my own. Fueled by those innocent dreams, I went north, where reality led me into the military. Although I had not anticipated taking that path, I accepted the challenges of military life. The small fears that fluttered in my stomach would fade. Tomorrow would be all right. Poppa had always promised me that. In spite of the struggles that Poppa and his friends endured, they always looked forward to the next day. They had experienced more fear and anxiety than I had ever known and still managed to nurture and shield us. They didn't become selfish or cease their dreaming. They embraced the future, and so would I. And if my background had caused me to be classified as a "bright boy," I knew it was because of them.

TWO

Classified,
Processed, Assigned

I arrived in Washington, D.C., in the spring. All that I had read about the nation's capital suddenly came to life as I became entranced with the historic monuments that greeted me from the banks of the Potomac. It almost felt like the same joy I had experienced as a child going to Greenville, Mississippi, with Poppa. We both loved the Queen City of the Delta, as Greenville was called.

My excitement was tempered by the knowledge that racial tensions had already bubbled over into violence. In the spring of 1966, black youngsters, turned away from an amusement park by a mob of angry whites, had vandalized a well-kept Washington neighborhood when they were forced to walk home. Then, that August, the pent-up frustrations of the poor in Washington's Anacostia district erupted in three hours of rock throwing, fire, and smoke— a minor riot that I saw televised at Dow.

My new assignment was taking me further and further away from Vietnam but closer to the conflict here at home, a conflict that had me and my people at its core. While at Dow, I was removed from the heat of urban fires and the stench of smoke-filled streets, but in Washington, with that struggle closer at hand, I would find my life developing dimensions I had not dreamed of as a child. The way I looked at life would subtly but profoundly change.

I had grown up in a small town where soldiers were romanticized and wars were rationalized. Not so here. The war was becoming more unpopular each day, and I watched as the numbers of public figures speaking out against the war increased. People that I respected—Julian Bond, Robert Kennedy, and others—were telling us that the war was wrong. I was immature and not sophisticated about the rights and wrongs of a war. Having just left Mississippi, I had not developed the voice of protest and questioning that would eventually characterize my South. It was the government's doing, so it must be right. I could not speak out. That would be like telling Poppa he was wrong. The voices of protest were loud and often confusing to me, so much so that it would take years for me to make my decision. Though I didn't know the historical context for the war, I knew innocent people were dying and that was wrong. Something had to be set right. And I knew that I wasn't on my way to Greenville anymore, with Poppa at the wheel. I was driving now, and I wasn't sure where the journey would lead. I was increasingly sure that it would not lead to Southeast Asia. However, there were other highways that I had not traveled but that I was drawn to by the powerful, gut-wrenching events of 1966 and 1967.

Washington had just about sidetracked me from Vietnam but not from the civil rights movement and its continuing growth in the South. I was hundreds of miles away from the Mississippi Delta, but in the months to come I would increasingly feel the heat of the struggle there. Tranquil pictures of Glen Allan's flowing lake and Greenville's Washington Avenue were being shattered by the sight of protest marchers and Freedom Riders, both unfamiliar to one who had grown up beneath the canopy of his elders' sheltering love.

This struggle was moving my elders closer to the freedom they had previously dreamed and spoken of only behind closed doors. During the days and months ahead, they would join a great battle. Across the South, the jailing of old folk suddenly grown strong would become commonplace. As in the days of slavery and the long years that followed, when black codes developed that gave birth to Jim Crow laws, their bodies would again become the canvas upon which their epitaphs were written in their blood. During those bad old days, you could pay with your life for any effort to claim your freedom or stand up for your rights.

Torn inside over my seemingly safe status, I nevertheless marched ahead to my assignment, the "good job" I had wanted so badly. Having received the assignment, I was now expected to live up to the epithet "bright boy." Although my attention was drawn to what was happening at home, the military had other plans for me. To them, I was a soldier, not a boy. They expected me to join the ranks and leave my personal life outside the gates. After all, I had been classified and assigned, and in spite of the world around me, they expected me to march on.

I arrived at Andrews Air Force Base at night, peering at what I could see of Washington in the dark as we drove through town and out toward the Maryland base. The next morning I would be processed. If I had learned anything at all since my days as a new recruit, it was the process of being processed—from filling out reams of paper to having my head shaved to bending over sterile white tables. Except for being spared the indignity of the shaved head and the white table, I knew that the tedium of being processed at Andrews would be much the same.

As I tried to relax in the guest housing, I summoned up the voices of the elders back home in Glen Allan who had spoken up for me, who believed in me, and whose memory would steady me as I began this new and more demanding aspect of my military life. I realized that in this place, despite the familiarity of certain routines, I would for all practical purposes be starting over again, meeting new commanders and noncommissioned officers, mastering new skills, and learning the unwritten rules for success at my new job.

Next morning, after processing, I was escorted to the Classified Section of the Eighty-ninth Supply Administration area to meet my new coworkers. I was determined to make a good impression. I was also determined to learn what these men knew and to gain their friendship and help. The building toward which we walked, behind a fenced-in classified area, had been polished till it shone, or so it appeared. The grounds were free of debris. When I was ushered into the office, each man looked like a military model in his well-pressed uniform. Some of the men smoked pipes; many moved briskly about. Except for Sgt. Myrick, all of them were white.

I was introduced to my superiors in the chain of command and was briefed on their expectations of me. I then met the noncommissioned officer, T.Sgt. Williams, who was directly in charge. He introduced me to the rest of the staff and showed me my desk. Then, as if to test this new "bright boy," he pelted me with questions. Before I could fully answer one, another came. Although inwardly I shook, I answered as quickly and precisely as I could. I still lived with the reality that my color had relegated me to an inferior position in society. And although I had been selected on my merits, I knew that if I failed, that failure would reflect on other blacks.

Because of this, I looked forward especially to Sgt. Myrick's acceptance and friendship. He had warmly welcomed me, and with my assignment to this unit, neither of us would be alone. I could bear with him the load of having to perform beyond official expectations. I was pleased to see that he had already secured a niche for himself. Except for the color of his skin, he looked and acted just like the others. I could tell from the responses of those around him that he knew his job. During my first few weeks, he privately shared with me the unspoken rules for achieving success at the Eighty-ninth. Our commander expected a lot from those assigned to this prestigious unit, and Sgt. Myrick made sure that I understood. Fortunately, it wasn't difficult for me to go beyond the expected; I had learned that lesson through hard work back home.

My work at Andrews, which was to include data processing, was more complicated than the work I had performed at Dow. For a while, I remained isolated, thinking almost solely about doing a good job and not worrying about the war that seemed to have no end or the civil rights movement that was growing more complex and rancorous as it moved north. I was easing into my role as a classified "bright boy," becoming proficient and gaining the respect of the men with whom I worked.

While students across America protested an "unjust war," I knew how lucky I was. Instead of carrying a rifle and slogging through a remote Southeast Asian swamp, I was safe, living in the city where the rights and wrongs of our involvement in Vietnam were hotly debated and where the civil rights movement had brought the cause for justice to the halls of Congress. But as I watched all of this from a safe remove, beholding a harvest in which I could not participate, I slowly became torn between my sense of duty and the promptings of my heart.

As I was coming to terms with the demands of my new job, my hometown, Glen Allan, and its sister towns across the South were moving forward with pain and travail. The system of legal segregation, which was supported by social mores as strong and deep as the piers that undergirded our democracy, was being challenged by a new breed of young southerners and their cousins from other regions who seemed determined to root out racism in all its forms. I read the stories. In many places beatings and jailings had become routine, but old black men and women were also standing up, stretching and reaching for all their rights. I knew the life from which they were emerging, and I had been told that one day change would come, but I never imagined that the price would be so high.

Except for tight security and the tall fence that locked us in and kept the world away, my working environment was not much different from what I had left at Dow. The walls were covered with charts and maps. There were no separate offices, and only the commander could shut his door. From his desk in the corner, T.Sgt. Williams could easily see both our office door and the commander's. Sgt. Myrick sat on the opposite side of the aisle, and my gray metal desk was positioned by the long blank wall, right in the path of traffic. We lived and worked in an environment that denied us privacy and individuality yet forced us together. At times there were bull sessions, but more often we went about our tasks, drank coffee, and kept our private thoughts to ourselves.

Nonetheless, the media reports on the civil rights movement created tensions that were heightened by our lack of walls. When bulletins about civil unrest reached our office, some of my older white coworkers grew quiet. Although we let the sounds of the typist and the constant ringing of the phones mask feelings that wanted out, I still heard the others' thoughts. And I am sure that they heard mine. Having no place to hide, I could only look down at the same document for so long. I had to raise my head, and when I did, I knew we needed to talk. I wanted to tell them that being black did not mean that I couldn't talk about my feelings or acknowledge theirs. Our world was "integrated," our uniforms were blue, and our color was thought to be secondary to our common goal; but we knew that it wasn't so on the outside, and in reality it wasn't so with us. So the subject of race just hung there like a cloud, while we made sure it didn't rain.

Most of the airmen seemed to agree on the good work being done by Dr. Martin Luther King Jr.—that is, until he spoke out against the war. Then they spoke up. Dr. King had stepped out of his role, they said, and he had not gotten their permission to do so: "Civil rights is one thing, but denouncing the war is something else." The more King spoke, the more we talked, but our talk seemed to lead nowhere. We could end our conversations, but we couldn't end the war. Instead, we made sure that life as we knew it went on. And I slowly found myself becoming a fixture like them, doing my job. With their help, I quickly began to complete my tasks independently and correctly, and later I found my adaptability valuable when assignments enhancing my chances for promotion came down the chain of command.

Because of the Eighty-ninth's position as a support unit to the president of the United States, we found ourselves learning state-of-the-art technology. Our unit had recently installed a well-secured cold room that held the new, mammoth IBM units. The old-timers, who had kept perfect card files for decades, saw no value in such a system, while the civilian operators prided and perhaps overrated themselves as our scientific and technological benefactors. Personally, I had enough to do and felt that such a system would not last; therefore, I didn't go out of my way to become familiar with the activities of the men in white who sat on the tall stools, handling disks, endless streams of paper, and massive stacks of punched cards. So engrossed were they in their world, they seemed to be the only people not aware of Vietnam and the civil rights movement. I guess they were launching their own offensives, ones called COBAL and FORTRAN.

Having become accustomed to the routine of my daily job, I was taken by surprise one day when I was told about a special project involving aircraft parts for the presidential fleet. The parts were kept at different strategic locations throughout the country, and those in command had decided that new locations were in order. We were never really told why, or at least I wasn't. Nevertheless, I was the one chosen to take on this major new assignment. T.Sgt. Williams guarded the task as if his life depended upon it, and he wanted my response to be the same. Because of its size and complexity, I became entirely focused on it for the next few weeks and had little time to think about the movement or the war.

At a time when the public at large knew very little about computer and data processing, they became part of my job. At first, I viewed computers as science fiction come alive. In my eagerness to be part of the team, to learn how to dismantle those remote supply storage areas, and to do it all by computer, I concealed my hesitancy and my fears. I was assured that using this tool of the future would be easy, but I felt a pressure that I wasn't about to let T.Sgt. Williams see. As he had explained, there were mistakes that could be rectified and there were mistakes that could change one's life, like sending the right "secret" part to the wrong place. Despite my fears, I knew that if I did this job well, it would look good on my record. I also wanted to prove that a black airman could do the job. I was determined that this assignment didn't need a white boy and could be done by me.

After I had received thorough instructions, I was left with this intimidating but exciting job of inventory movement and reassignment of the presidential aircraft parts. As I completed the inventory sheets and the corresponding punch cards, I made daily visits to the computer room. In the midst of bells sounding and doors closing, I began to feel at home, just as I had adjusted to the cash register when I worked as a youngster at Mr. Hilton's grocery store.

Mr. Hilton's cash register had once been out of reach to coloreds. We could clean the store, sack the groceries, and cut the meat—all of which I learned to do—but the big silvery cash register was strictly Mrs. Hilton's domain. She guarded it as though it were top secret, wiping the dust off the keys and shining the chrome-plated body. Even Mr. Hilton rarely stepped behind the counter. When no customers were in the store, Mrs. Hilton just sat on a tall stool and watched the register glow, waiting for the next person to come, buy food, and pay homage to this mysterious machine. When someone did come in, she would ease her sizable body off the stool and stand right beside the register, as if she and the register were ready for anything.

Sometimes when I brought the meat I had cut to the front, I cautiously watched as she let her fingers fly over the keys and then looked into the face of the customer. "More for you?" she would inquire, and if the answer was "no," she would hit the total key, bells would ring, the drawer would slide out, and she would push the money in. I wanted that experience. Growing up in Poppa's house had made me believe I could do anything on which I set my sights. Although we had little materially, Poppa Joe and Mama Pearl Young, my great-grandparents, always made us feel we could do important things. I could sit up front in church because I was Poppa's boy. In the fields, I got the coveted job of "water boy," watching the big bucket and all through the day providing cool drinks of water to the hot field hands. Of course, I got that job because I was Ma Ponk's nephew. She was a community leader, looked up to and treated nicely, even in the fields. I was a beneficiary of her position. I represented my school in 4-H Club rallies and learned to change the tractor oil in a 4-H competition. I grew up wanting to be involved in those things that made people take notice of you.

Maybe it was my longing eyes or my cautious, momentary pauses to watch, but I finally got my turn. It was a grand day. Mrs. Hilton approached my training like a technical school veteran. I was pumped full of information on the keys, especially the total key. Now I could stand behind the front counter—not to sack meat or groceries but to operate the cash register. I was scared. Mrs. Hilton watched my every move, as did Mr. Hilton, who came up front from the kitchen in the back of the store. Of course, my first customer was a colored person, and seeing me behind the counter was as startling for him as it was for me to find myself standing there. It was a moment to savor and a time to remember. With the groceries in front of me, I carefully keyed them in, then I looked up: "More for you? No?" I hit the total key, the drawer slid out, and I triumphantly put the money in. I had succeeded! I would succeed again. Of course, I quickly found that working the register was going to be easy, and I understood that it certainly did not warrant the laborious instructions I had been given. But being up front made me feel good and important, and it somehow validated the confidence of our teachers that their best students were capable of so much more than field work.

Over the course of my first big assignment at Andrews, all of the airplane parts under my control were safely transferred to their intended destinations; and when T.Sgt. Williams, who was not known for giving out compliments, praised me for a job well done, I felt great. "Poppa's little boy" from the Delta had "done good," just as he had at Hilton's store. I had had the same feeling when I picked my first two hundred pounds of cotton—a feat that happened only once—and my stepfather had given me a Dreamsicle as my reward. Although I had eaten those orange and vanilla ice cream bars as long as I could recall, this was the first time my father had bought one for me, just for doing a man's job. It was a reward I cherished.

My completion of the special assignment—in which I

used technology that was new and did well—was also cause for a reward. My timely and accurate completion of the job had reflected favorably on our entire unit. T.Sgt. Williams requested that I be allowed to go on a special guided tour of Air Force One, the plane that served the president of the United States.

This was something I had always wanted to do, especially since it would put me on equal footing with the other men in my unit, all of whom had already made the tour. Also, ever since I had entered the service, folk always asked whether I had been on Air Force One. Now that I served in the unit that serviced and maintained the fleet, the questions were even more frequent. With some difficulty, I had to explain that Air Force One didn't sell tickets; it was not TWA. Still, I was expected to know how it looked inside and all the details of its custom styling and design. Not having the heart to say that I had only seen the plane parked from a distance, I kept my questioners at bay by telling them that, given time, my name would come up and I would be invited to inspect the "White House with wings."

T.Sgt. Williams came over to my desk one day, smoking his ever-present pipe, looking around as if he saw something that no one else recognized. "Well, Sgt. Taulbert, on next Monday, around eleven hundred hours, be ready, polished, and all; you'll be going on a tour of Air Force One." I could hardly contain my excitement. Even before I arrived at Andrews, my friends at Dow had filled my head with stories about Air Force One. Before I enlisted, I had never thought about the president's mode of travel. However, many of my friends had long been aware of the plane and, when they found out I was being assigned to Andrews, were eager to share their excitement with me. Suddenly it seemed as though every other person I knew had a friend, cousin, or brother who had been in the Secret Service, had worked on the plane, or was assigned to security and, because of these connections, knew the kinds of food served on the plane, the kinds of passengers it carried, the places it went, and how fast it flew. I had savored every detail. And now here were Sgt. Myrick and T.Sgt. Williams offering their own descriptions of the plane's grandeur and state-of-the-art gadgets. It was bigger, they said, than my hometown of Glen Allan and nicer than Greenville. Of course, they had never seen either place. I myself began comparing the plane's majesty to that of Lake Washington back home, which shimmered like a giant silver bird beneath the Delta sun.

When Monday morning came I was up early, fighting for a place at the sink in the crowded john. I wanted to look my best, and this was the day to do it. Not only did the air force require that we look sharp, but Sgt. Myrick had told me that colored airmen were carefully monitored for neatness and polish, and there was no doubt that I would be noticed on Air Force One. I had spit shined my shoes to a high gloss, my summer uniform was carefully pressed, my teeth were scrubbed, and my hair was brushed to my scalp. Nothing would be out of place. I was wide awake, determined to set a standard that day.

Later, as we approached the plane, the gleaming presidential emblem reflected my mood. The eagle looked regal. The blue was the brightest I had ever seen. The MPs who protected the plane stared straight ahead as we passed. "Move quickly, Sergeant," one of the men urged as I took my time walking up the steps. I savored each step, slowly ducking my head under the arched opening. Finally, I was in. I stared at the beautifully appointed interior. They were right, it was grand. From living room to sleeping quarters, I touched everything twice, making sure I would never forget this up-close visit. Then, as I meandered through the conference room, a single red telephone caught my eye.

I looked at the phone, which sat by itself on a highly polished table. There was no one else in the room; they were all in the cockpit and in other areas of the plane. I was not interested in cockpit controls, but I was hypnotized by the phone. Could it be hooked up to Moscow? As I slowly crossed the room, the phone seemed to pull me to it, begging me to pick up the receiver. But who would answer? Surely not the Soviet premier! If not him, who would? As I leaned toward the phone, I could see my face reflected in the receiver handle. What would happen, I wondered, as I slowly extended my right hand. At that moment my reverie was shattered by a bellowing voice: "Okay, men, let's clear out." I dropped my hand and quickly joined the others, casting one look back at the phone.

If I could count on anyone to understand my excitement over the phone, it would be Sgt. Myrick. In fact, my story amused him very much. Places that had the grandeur of Air Force One, I explained, had been off-limits to me as I was growing up in the South. He laughed when I told him how standing over the red phone had given me a chance to get even with Mrs. Johnson, who ruled the post office in Glen Allan and often made us colored kids feel insignificant. I showed him how she would look straight through you while recognizing a white person who had just entered the post office. I was mesmerized by her stamp machine and could stand all day just listening to it go "thump," making each letter official. She managed the post office from a caged window, a place where only Mr. Antiseptic, the old colored man who cleaned the place, was allowed to go. But I was determined one day to touch the stamper and sit on Mrs. Johnson's stool. And I did.

It happened one day when Mr. Antiseptic was sick, and I was hired to fill in for him. I couldn't believe my good fortune! As I thoroughly oiled the old wooden floor, Mrs. Johnson stepped outside the building to wait for the oil to dry. The minute she was gone, I climbed up on her stool, seized the stamper, and, to my heart's delight, thumped postmarks on scraps of paper. If only for a moment, I had felt a surge of power, just as I had on Air Force One.

All in all, I felt very happy to be at the Eighty-ninth,

where my expectations for my job were high, and where I could count on Sgt. Myrick to be my friend. I felt that my success with the special computer job would land me more of the same, and I was beginning to feel at home. However, my one great disappointment at Andrews was the barracks, which were nothing like the barracks my buddies and I had imagined in our weekend talks at Dow. The building where I now lived was one story with a single entry, and its exterior was old with peeling paint.

The large recreation room held a few overstuffed chairs that faced the wall. When I first saw it, I paused for a moment trying to imagine activity, but it was stark and lifeless, unlike the one at Dow. As I walked down the hall and saw the large, open community john, my heart sank. At Dow there had been at least one john for every two rooms, but not here. And then there was my room. I had dreamed of a big room with a private john and a real wall with curtains, but this one was cramped, the built-in closets were small, the chairs were hard, and the two plain beds were built into the walls.

Still, as I reminded myself more than once, there were compensations. If my living quarters were not what I wanted, they were also not in Vietnam. And the two guys across the hall became my friends. Over time, they tried to teach me to gamble, chase women, and drink wine. Although I liked them both, the fears instilled in me by Ma Ponk won out. I didn't have the makings of a party animal.

My excuses didn't bother them, though, and we remained good friends.

As time passed, this base and the shabby barracks gradually became a place I could call home. It would never be what I really wanted, and it would never replace the home where I was reared, but it eventually became a retreat, the place where I could go, hit the walls, read a book, or be hurt or scared all by myself. And when I lay down to sleep, I wasn't afraid. I heard no bombs, nor did Molotov cocktails explode outside my door. I got used to the community john, just as I did the shared number three washtub in which we bathed back home. And the quiet, underused recreation room that I didn't like at first became an oasis, the place where I went to write, look out the window, and remember the faces and the smiles of the people who were still counting on me to do well and make them proud.

As the events of the day continued to shape my world, I realized that the home I knew as a child was more than the house Grandpa built, it was the love I felt while living in the house, a feeling that was transportable. It could be with me, even here, hundreds of miles away as my world changed and as I contemplated what was happening there. It was clear to me, too, what really happened when I left home with my elders' blessing, pointed in the direction where I dreamed that freedom lived. I had said goodbye to them all from the windows of the train, and they had walked away with a resolve that ushered in the change I now watched from afar. I had thought them to be my cheering section as I left for the war. Not so. They would become the soldiers, and fighting for my future would become their war. I was uniformed and trained, but they were marching into battle.

VOTE NOVEMBER 7
FOR

Clarence HALL, Jr.

SUPERVISOR
BEAT FOUR
ISSAQUENA COUNTY

If You Vote For Me I Will
Work For You
THANK YOU!

GREENVILLE
GLEN ALLAN
HOLLANDALE

1 436

THREE

When Saturday Night Met Sunday Morning

By the time early fall arrived, I was in a state of great excitement. I was going home on leave. My work at the base had become easy, and I had a few weeks before classes began at the University of Maryland, where I had started in the spring to carry as many night courses as I could in history, philosophy, and English. I would be at home one week. Although I was restless to see my family and friends again, and to see what was happening at home, I also wondered if I would encounter trouble. Would I be considered an outside agitator, or would my uniform shield me from possible harm? In years past, southerners, black and white, had been respectful of the military, a tradition I hoped would still be in place.

Many people in Glen Allan were engaged in a battle in which their lives were on the line. As the battle progressed, they were changing Glen Allan and helping to create a new South. Media stories about the civil rights movement had captured almost as much attention as the war. On top of that, everything seemed to have happened so quickly. One day we all sat listening to the news, and then, before we knew it, we had become the news.

The old blues men often sang of leaving the South for Chicago, taking nothing but a dream and the clothes on their backs. Very few sang of coming home, but they came back nonetheless. For years they had returned to a familiar South, where traditions were rooted deeply in the Delta soil. They knew what to expect and who to watch out for. And so had I when I came home for a visit two years before. Now, things would be different back home.

I had to take the bus from Washington, D.C., to Glen Allan. Passenger trains no longer ran, and I didn't have a car. The buses were integrated now, which meant that the Greenville bus station would be integrated, too. I had seen integration before, but not at home, and I didn't know to what extent it had been implemented. I did know, however, that life-long traditions were changing as a result of the civil rights movement, and I expected that all I would probably see would be a room in the bus station that no longer bore the designation "colored." For years, I thought, my people had dreamed and struggled for a change that simply required the removal of a pasteboard sign.

I had never liked the bus. Ma Ponk had always told me to ride the train, the high-class mode of travel. But the railroads forgot to get Ma Ponk's permission to stop running the passenger trains, and I now found myself crowded into a bus with whites and blacks, all of us wrapped in an uneasy quiet as we traveled a familiar route. I was on my way home to the Delta.

Since my mother had not yet purchased a car or learned to drive, I was met at the bus by her oldest brother, Johnny. Highway One, which took us from Greenville to Glen Allan, had not changed. Cotton fields lined both sides, just as they had when I was a boy. I sat quietly in the car as we passed familiar scenes—Lake Washington, Marathon Plantation, Linden, and Wildwood. I saw no change until we got close to Glen Allan. Telephone poles were plastered with civil rights posters and notices, and uptown there was a lot of activity—not a soul sat on the loafers' bench, the bench where old colored people usually sat and waited and watched. Both blacks and whites had benches in the sun, and all who sat there were called loafers, probably because people reasoned that in a country where everyone worked so hard only the "lazy" and the "no account" would find time to sit and while the hours away. But the loafers' bench was more than that to us. It was our little piece of uptown. From the loafers' bench we could watch the world file in and out of Glen Allan. Today, the bench was empty, and I saw people milling around that I didn't know. Stranger still was the sight of white people walking around in our neighborhood, which really confirmed for me the changes that the media had caught.

As we drew nearer to Ma Ponk's home, I was relieved to see her standing on her front porch, just as I knew she would be. Some things never changed. In keeping with family tradition, I had to see her first, receive my visiting instructions, and let her show me the room where I would sleep. Although I was her boy, I was now also her guest. After we had talked, we walked together down the narrow hall to "Sidney's room," which had belonged to Ma Ponk's youngest son. It held the good wooden furniture, which sat on floral linoleum, the sewing machine that was never used, and college pictures of Sidney and his wife, Bea. Ma Ponk had raised both windows to air out the room, turned back the bedcovers, and placed the towels at the foot of the bed. While I was unpacking, I could feel the fall wetness in the air. As I touched the sheets, the Delta dampness reached up to welcome me. I was home, and here was Ma Ponk handing me a glass of my favorite cold mint tea.

As I finished unpacking and walked up the hall past Ma Ponk's bedroom, she said, "Be careful now, 'cause the whites ain't like they used to be, with the movement and all. Spike Ayers is heavily involved. He done seen some trouble, but I am on my knees for him eber night." Ma

Ponk was making sure I understood that the carefully orchestrated social order we had known all our lives had changed and that Sidney's best friend, Jake Ayers, whom everyone at home called Spike, was a leader of that change.

In the days that followed, I saw this great change for myself. The movement, like the military, had brought together people who had formerly stood apart. In this new configuration, upstanding folks worked alongside the people we called "sinners" when I was growing up—people who were known for their transgressions, who were singled out, and who usually stayed within their ranks. The juke joints were their places of worship. For them, the churches were simply places to get married and later to be "funeralized," while the churches saw these people as potential trophies, prizes to be sought, souls to be saved, but never working partners. The movement had changed all that. All the able-bodied were being enlisted, and the saints and sinners were drawn together into the fields.

Known "men and women of the night" who had gambled, drunk, and chased after the loves of their lives were now polished and committed. Mr. K. C. Mapp, who loved to gamble and always dressed like a gentleman, was in charge of transportation for the Head Start center; Jesse Jones, who loved fishing, hunting, and a little gambling, was involved; and the wild-mannered Miss Gussie was heading up the cleaning crew and would substitute as a driver when needed. Especially prominent was Spike

Ayers, who earlier was among the unchurched but had now become a leader in the fight.

What was even more amazing to me was that these people had stepped forward just at a time when there was a need for a different type of person—one who had fortitude and guts enough to battle the system and not care. Such people were not originally found in churches. Instead, it was the denizens of the juke joints who could not only gamble and curse and drink you under the table but could also stand up in public and be counted. Miss Gussie, who daily drove the school bus better than any man, was a Saturday night brawler in her bright red lipstick and skin tight dress. Now she also drove people to vote. She had become a political activist under the tutelage of Spike Ayers.

The churches had become the meeting places for all involved, and the once off-limits juke joints were now catering food and serving as message centers. The movement had been birthed to ensure democracy for all regardless of race, but it was also transforming the people of Glen Allan into a vital single unit. As the movement made room for all, leaders emerged from among the ranks who were able to ignore lines that had been drawn long before I was born. In short, the movement was destroying many of our old traditions, and not just the ones that separated white and black.

Without all working together, crossing lines to hold hands, the voter registration drives could not have been so successful, and the seeds for Head Start, which came after the first intense period of political activism in 1964, would not have been planted. This effective coalition of neighbors and friends looked to Spike Ayers and others to keep them melded together.

They were making headway. They were getting grants, people were getting jobs, citizens were voting for the very first time, and they had begun prepping the children for the future. Still I knew that this war would not easily be won. Because I had a safe assignment in Washington, my life was not on the line, but their lives were and they volunteered anyway. I saw them, the ordinary people I knew, becoming the committed and the brave. I also talked with some of the volunteers who worked side by side with them. Many were young and idealistic, but upon their idealism and the courage of old dreamers a movement that challenged America and changed the South was being born.

When I had left Glen Allan in May of 1963, the town was still legally segregated. I had never been able to check out a book from the public library. Although I had vague memories of a cottonfield friendship between a teenaged white boy, myself, and another colored kid from the colony, what I was seeing now was altogether different. In broad daylight, I saw young white men sitting on empty soda cases talking with black men. They were laughing together. They were sharing their lives. And they didn't seem to be afraid. Young white lawyers with their sleeves rolled up and their faces red from the baking sun were walking from house to house, while Frank Hudson, a young black man I had known all my life, connected them with the people who needed legal assistance. Miss Fannie Loving was housing them, and the juke joints were feeding them.

When I was home before, we had quietly discussed our hopes among ourselves, but I had not experienced what I witnessed now—blacks and whites working together for social change. That had not been part of my world. While I was away being trained to fight for democracy in Vietnam, Glen Allan changed. Volunteers of all kinds came. Some were southern whites, but many were students with long hair and Afros from back east. As in the military, I saw them all working together without regard for the potential loss of life. They had not come south as part of an intellectual exchange; they had come to work, and they knew the dangers they would face.

Before my trip home, I had thought that most of the white visitors would be media people, not committed volunteers. After all, Ma Ponk in her letters always described them as white folks with pony tails and cameras who ran around taking pictures of everything and everybody. But their involvement was real. Even the deaths in Mississippi of the three civil rights workers slain in 1964—Andrew Goodman, Michael Schwerner, and James Cheney—could not frighten them away. They kept coming. Their quickness to roll up their sleeves and become like us surprised many, although Poppa had always said that white people would get better sooner or later. And as I saw white people mingling in our heretofore segregated world, I thought of Elder Thomas, our pastor at St. Mark's Missionary Baptist Church. Years before, when I was a child, he had vividly described a dream of his that suddenly seemed relevant to what we were witnessing now.

I was remembering that dream on my way to visit Cousin Beauty. But I decided to stop first at St. Mark's, where I had spent most of my young life seated on the mourners' bench, the place where sinners confessed to the community and prayed for divine intervention. From the outside, St. Mark's looked the same, except that the faded white paint was now a faded gray. I looked up. Yes, the old bell was still there. It used to ring all the time but seldom rang anymore, I was told, which was all right with me. I had never really liked it because the deacons always sounded it in solemn tones to let us know when someone died.

Now, in the midst of so much activity and racial unrest, I was surprised to find the church door open. I walked in and stood at the back. It was quiet, almost eerie, as I looked around at all the empty chairs. No padded pews, just the same wooden folding chairs I had sat in as a boy. The same velvet picture of the Last Supper hung on the wall, and each seat held a funeral home fan. I was glad that not much here had changed.

Even the old wooden pulpit was as I remembered it, though it looked much smaller. It had seemed massive when I was a child. Now I could look over it and see out the back windows. I had grown up. As I recalled how powerful the pulpit had seemed back then and how big Elder Thomas had looked when he stood up and preached, I remembered a service from long ago. The sermon that day was not the usual one in which Elder Thomas thundered at the crowd. In fact, it may have been the only quiet sermon he ever preached.

As I sat on the front row in the empty church, I could once again see Elder Thomas's tall, imposing body slowly rising from the preacher's chair to tower over the old wooden pulpit. He spoke gently, drawing us in, as he told of a dream he had had that he felt must be shared with all of us. "Gawd done showed me that we'se in his number," he said. "We got a place. In my dream ther wuz angels coming all around me, more than I could eber count. Yes ser, they wuz white ones and colored ones, flying all together. They wuz comin to talk wit me. I couldn't wait to hear them, but as they got almost to me, and I raised up to listen, something woke me up. I don't know the meaning. But I do know that Gawd was trying to tell me somethin'." As Elder Thomas went on to preach that a change was coming and no man would be able to stop it, amens and shouts rang out through the old church.

Now, years later, I thought that just maybe Elder Thomas had seen the Freedom Riders in his dream. He didn't live to see the great gathering that swept across the

South into Glen Allan, but the people did come; the black ones and the white ones came, and I had seen their work.

Some of those young people who came to my home-town were among America's brightest. From their lips, many of the old black people heard whites for the first time call them "Mr." and "Mrs." Because those youth believed that brotherhood was obtainable, they were loved by some, welcomed by many, and cursed by those to whom they were "outsiders," come to stir up trouble. Their guide was Spike Ayers, who instructed them in the ways of the South. When they became discouraged at the slow pace of progress, he was there to keep them focused. He treasured their youth and vitality, and in him they found a true comrade.

While at home, I learned more about the real Spike Ayers than I had ever gleaned from the media stories. The stories, which focused on his confrontations with the white power structure, captured his fire, but at home I also saw the works of his heart. As he organized our commu-nity politically and also worked to get Head Start going in the Delta, many of the local whites called him an agitator, a man who would not leave well enough alone. As his role expanded, there were threats against his life.

Spike's fervor, commitment, and ability to communicate made him the logical choice to voice the people's con-cerns. He seemed to lack fear and had gained a reputation as a straight talker, even to government leaders like Sargent Shriver, the boss at the Office of Economic Opportunity. The OEO was especially important, because it had become the financial umbilical cord for Project Head Start. Spike didn't hesitate to tell Shriver and the others what he felt they needed to do about funding programs to help the Delta poor. As a result, the press was quick to seize upon this new face, a grass-roots leader, and bring him to the attention of the nation.

I read about him in Washington and watched him on the evening news. When they photographed him, they made sure his large salt-and-pepper Afro dominated the picture. He had the reputation of barging right into the offices of power in Washington, disregarding their protocol while maintaining his cool diplomacy. He looked them right in the eye and spoke his mind. Without question, a new Glen Allan was being born and Spike Ayers was personifying the new black voice.

As I was growing up, Washington, D.C., had always been "that place way out yonder," the place where the president and his people lived. Even though we envisioned most of the people there as white, we also felt that in small ways we had benefited from their measured benevolence. Washington was the one place we felt to be our court of last resort, the place where justice lived. For that reason, I now found it difficult to believe that an ordinary citizen, a colored man from Glen Allan, could look at the national political establishment from all sides and publicly distinguish the truth from a well-placed lie. After all, the people he stood up to held the purse strings to the movement's much-needed funding. But stand up to them he did. So genuine was Spike's love for our town and its people that he knowingly put his life on the line to make sure their story was told. He had only one agenda: trying to make life better for his people.

Spike Ayers was not my contemporary; he was from my mother's generation, but I knew him. I knew his parents also. His father, who was one of the early colored straw bosses, had managed Miss Spencer's large plantation. As a child, I thought he was white because he was so light-skinned. The Ayerses raised their children to be part of the community, yet I never figured Spike to be a leader. However, he later proved that his heart and life were insepa-rable from the people. The old people said he was "called." They said if you are "called" you can't get away from it. Some said he got caught up in the intensity of the move-ment and couldn't back out, but those who really knew him felt he was born to represent the dreams of his people.

I knew Spike had started college at Mississippi's Alcorn A and M because I had seen a picture of him there with Sidney, Ma Ponk's son. Later, after Spike had dropped out, he always visited our house when Sidney came home on break. Although their lives took separate paths, Spike and Sidney remained friends, and during the summer and semester breaks, they would get together for Jax beer, fried catfish, and white perch. They enjoyed those visits, and I remembered them.

Maybe Spike was a leader in the making even then. After dropping out of college he had chances to go north like many others, but he stayed home and each year became more anchored to the community and more troubled by its problems. He respected the strength and resolve shown by his elders, but he wanted more. He wanted full citizenship, the right to vote, and integrated schools. When he saw hunger, he wanted the children fed. He said if we could feed the Vietnamese, we could certainly take care of our own. While the rest of us went north, off to college or the military, he stayed behind, watching and observing our hometown. And when the civil rights movement finally penetrated the cotton curtain, the community was ready for his leadership. As an emerging leader, he was seeing his future through the lengthening steps of the children and the grandchildren. His yard, his porch, and his home had become their gathering places. He was becoming their elder.

Ma Ponk's letters had told me how Spike's front yard would be overrun with men and women who had no other place to discuss their political views and their hopes for the future. When I came home, I saw it for myself. I saw the tenant farmers who feared open expression at their homes, but at Spike's house they talked freely. I saw them propped up on soda water boxes, sitting cross-legged on the ground, and perched atop cars. This congregation of newly formed political activists listened to his plans while being fueled by his courage. He rattled the fences of tradition while trying to build bridges to the future. The young people admired him. The old people trusted him. And I sensed that this man, with his hair prematurely turning white, was beginning a journey that would last the rest of his life.

I had never seen colored people with so many important-looking papers to read or have read to them. But Spike was determined that they know everything. For the first time in their lives, many were learning about their basic rights and privileges under the constitution. Whatever Spike didn't know, he had young college activists ready to explain. His old screen door never stood still; someone was always coming in or going out. On the day that I first stopped by to pay my respects, Spike cut a striking figure in the midst of all the people gathered at his house, with his yellow-skinned face framed by a larger-than-life Afro. He had a pencil stuck behind his ear and glasses sat on his nose. "Just like a straw boss," I thought as I waited to say hello. Even though he was obviously busy, he stopped to speak, shake my hand, and chat for a few moments with me.

Few expected national leaders to rise from the ranks of those born in the little cotton communities located throughout the South. However, during the 1960s, so profound was the emergence of ordinary field hands and domestic workers into positions of leadership that it seemed as if new voices were being heard almost daily, reminding us of what we had left to do. Spike Ayers was right there among them. Glen Allan had birthed one whose commitment to the ordinary people and their children would make his life cast a giant shadow, one that would reach beyond the Delta, even to Washington, D.C.

I thought it fitting that Spike's small frame house had once been the home of Callie Mae Ballard and her husband, Mr. Boot-Nanny. Miss Callie Mae was one of Glen Allan's midwives and, like Spike, had dedicated her life to our lives. No matter the time of night, if she was needed, she would come. Sending instructions back to get the water boiling, tear the sheets in strips, and hang quilts at the windows, she ushered in new life. And now here was Spike Ayers, often answering late-night calls to advance the work of freedom. Both knew the joy waiting at the end of the labor, and both were acutely aware of the dangers that accompanied delivery. As I thought about the irony of place, people, and time, I thought I could hear Miss Callie Mae's voice mingling with Spike's: "It might pain you now, gal, but don't give up. Hold on, 'cause it'll be joy in the morning." "Pain," I thought. Both Spike and Miss Callie knew the dangers of their work, but they were also moved by helping to bring dreams and visions to full term.

For Spike, a very real danger arose from the Klan, and I admired his commitment and respected his bravery all the more, knowing about the Klan's agenda to run him off or scare him into quitting. But in spite of their verbal threats and efforts to humiliate him, he didn't run. He didn't quit. He held his ground. As a soldier, I had fear that I'd be sent to Vietnam, but those orders never came. I never saw the enemy I feared, but Spike encountered his enemy daily, and so did his family.

Growing up in Glen Allan, I had never personally seen the racism that hid behind sheets and traveled by night. I never saw a burning cross, only the charred remains of the *Delta Democrat Times* editor, who had been burned in effigy in our small, all-white park. While I was working and going to school, and American soldiers were dodging the Vietcong in jungle camouflage, Spike, his wife, Lillie, and their young children encountered an enemy fueled by ignorance, fear, and hate working their vengeance by night.

Ma Ponk told me about the Klan and their attempt to scare Spike and Lillie. She said it happened before anybody got the word and could send help. Keeping to Klan tradition, they arrived just about midnight. Driving old pickups, yelling curses and insults, and carrying a burning cross, they rode into Glen Allan. With the adults were young white boys, too young to really know what they were doing as they followed their elders into colored town. Bearing a burning cross and chanting a gospel not meant for salvation, they invaded the Ayerses' personal world. They tossed their "calling card" cross into Spike's small yard, right next door to the St. Mark's Missionary Baptist Church. As quickly as they came, they left. Only the burning cross and fear were left behind. But Glen Allan coloreds were survivors; they had outlived charred crosses before and had even survived the hurt of kin being killed and hanged, and so would Spike Ayers and his family survive. This was but one battle in a war that wasn't over.

I wished that Poppa had been alive to see the freedom of expression I witnessed. Poppa had prayed for this day, and so had many of his friends as they dared to dream of a place in time when all of God's children were welcome to share the same sun. Though he was deceased, I did go by his home, my place of birth, to visit Miss Sissy, the lady he married after Mama Pearl passed away. Miss Sissy was nice to us, but the place wasn't the same without Poppa. The long front porch was there, but the rocking chair was gone. And there were no gatherings of preachers holding court and no Mama Pearl passing out slices of her red jelly cake, a layered cake that southerners whipped up for everyday occasions. I wished them to be there as I sat for a moment on the top steps and looked back into a front room that was filled with my memories of old black men.

Poppa's front room was always filled with Baptist preachers and their head deacons. They always seemed to have traveled in pairs, and Poppa's house was their safe place. There in the large front room they held court, their version of a town hall meeting. I watched in innocence and listened as the old preachers took turns talking about "the change" that they knew would one day come. All the old Baptist preachers knew each other and often got together to talk among themselves about social conditions and the inequities their people faced. Elder Thomas was a respected member of this group, and no doubt he spoke to them at length about the vivid dream he had told us of in church and the hope it promised.

They were all dreamers, and they longed for the day when the young visionaries would come. They took the Bible literally and believed that God gave old men dreams but placed the visions in the hearts of the young. While they talked, moaned, and prayed, Mama Pearl went about the business of making them comfortable. She never appeared to be overly concerned about what she called "men's business"; she just made sure that Poppa was all right and seated in the big horsehair chair that sat by the door to their small bedroom. Armed with hot cups of coffee and slices of red jelly cake, she quietly hummed her way through the gathering of men as they talked among themselves and reminded their God of their plight.

They came in worn shiny suits and white shirts yellowed with age from old tobacco stains and snuff juice that rainwater couldn't get out. They smelled of Old Spice and sported worn-out Stacy Adam shoes, which had been sent to them, used, by relatives who had moved north. These shoes were expensive and hard to get and were treasured and worn forever as signs of "success."

Only the old screen door separated me from these men who talked about a world they could see and hear but could not touch and feel. Through that door I heard them agonize over the injustice of the low pay they received for their work in the fields—for they were both clergymen and field hands—and the lack of respect shown by young white boys who spoke down to them. I never heard them complain about the segregated schools, only about the way some of the plantations kept young colored kids out of school to work in the fields. Although they never resorted to violence, their voices reflected their feelings of hurt about being cheated of the land and life that their God had promised to all men. All of their lives they had worked the land, but the system had kept much of the harvest from benefiting them.

I also heard their stinging choruses of accusations against politicians they had not elected. Although kept from active political participation, they seemed to have known those politicians who had twisted the laws to benefit the whites. Even so, they respected the law and prayed for the lawbreakers. They would slap their hands on their knees, stomp their feet, and raise their voices; their congress was in session, but no legislative action could be taken.

Preacher Hurn, from the colored colony, was always there. The whites thought he was crazy, but he was an intellectual before his time. He spoke of independence when few understood its value. Coming from an area of Issequana County where black people were self-sufficient, he was not dependent on the plantation structure for his livelihood. Uncle Abe Brown also joined them. He had read extensively, and although he was not allowed to participate in the government of his town, he was known as book smart among the coloreds. Sometimes Poppa's preacher friends from Greenville would also come down, but mostly it was a gathering of country preachers, voicing their opinions behind closed doors. They knew how to right the wrongs and even how to make the crops yield more, but no one in power cared to ask their opinion. They ate the jelly cake, drank the coffee, and always prayed. Later Mama Pearl would come through, still humming, pick up the empty plates and cups and beckon for me to come in and get my piece of cake.

Poppa and his friends had recognized their limitations in the place they called home. I was now watching as some of their dreams were coming true. Some of the old preachers had taken conversations from Poppa's living room into their pulpits and had helped begin the social revival that eventually became the movement now sweeping the South. When I was a boy, only Mr. Joe Maxey, his wife, the colored principal, and the pastor of the local colored Methodist Church ventured to vote, but now young people were being raised up full of strength and resolve, and they were forcing the law of the land to apply to my hometown.

No more $3.00 a day for back-breaking labor. After all, our people were citizens, too. The young people had grasped the full meaning of citizenship early on. They had gained a basic understanding of the Constitution, the Declaration of Independence, and the Bill of Rights, and they knew that the time had come to make their knowledge a community reality. The federal government had finally responded, and the laws were being challenged in court to ensure justice and support equality. The power of the black vote was being acknowledged as white candidates slowly came around to enlist the support of the community. Poppa's hometown would never be the same again, and I wished I could tell him and his friends that their God had finally heard, and I was seeing his answers all around.

FOUR

Smothered Steak
and Kool-Aid

Of all the changes I witnessed on my visit home, none would have pleased Poppa and his old friends more than the role and accomplishments of my mother, Mary, in Project Head Start. Many of the plain and ordinary citizens of our community had now been mobilized under the leadership of people like Spike and Lillie Ayers, and others like those from the independent colored farming communities and colored professionals had stepped forward as well. Call them field workers or troops, I was amazed at the gathering of leaders that had emerged in such a short time.

Bud Hall from Valewood was intimately involved, a stalwart spokesman, a political man in the making. When I left home, Bud was an independent farmer. I rarely saw him in town except on weekends, but now this tall, dignified man appeared to have stored his tractor in the shed, donned new work clothes, and joined the others in the social justice field.

The women were there as well, and none was more present than Unita Blackwell, whom I never really knew except in pictures and from the stories others told. She had lived in and around Glen Allan most of her life, and she was hardly anyone that we would have expected to rise so quickly to national prominence. But something had struck a spark in this tall, dark lady, and she had appeared out of the countryside determined to be part of the effort to make life better for the people she knew and loved. It seemed as though one day she was a neighbor from down the road and the next day she was a guest at the White House. A citizen of Rolling Rock and Mayersville, she eventually became Mississippi's first black female mayor. But then she was just one of the new voices of the Delta determined to be heard.

Another voice was my mother's. She was not political, but she had heard a summons to teach and she had answered. Mama had been working in the kitchen of the white football and basketball coach at Glen Allan's previously all-white high school when that summons came. She had always loved teaching, and now, having heard of the newly developing Head Start program, she had found her chance to resume that calling. Laying aside her apron and all that it stood for, she went to the University of Alabama for special Head Start administrative training, which opened the door to a new career as director of the Yates Head Start Center. Although she had written me often about these changes and had sent me clippings about Head Start from the *Greenville Delta Democrat Times*, now that I was home I could hardly wait to see for myself what was happening.

While in Washington, I had become captive to the media and their tendency to exploit every sensational story of suffering and loss in the South. Although we needed to know about that suffering, the instances of personal loss, and the ever-present menace of the Klan, we also needed to know the stories of the people's resiliency and resolve that made the struggle bearable and gave it meaning. Lost jobs, workers forced off the plantations, beatings, and the burning of black people's homes were vivid parts of the struggle, but so was the emergence of hope. Head Start provided a haven where children could begin to change their futures, and my mother's letters about it always brightened my day. Captivated by her work, she was deeply involved in the lives of the families she served, and she had experienced a wonderful turn-around in her personal life. With Head Start, she resumed the kind of work she had done when I was small, teaching school at the Peru Plantation. She had made that old church school a warm and wonderful place. And now, she was creating the same kind of environment at Head Start.

On my first night at home, after visiting Ma Ponk, I went across the road to see my mother. As I walked into her front yard, I could smell her cooking in the evening air. It was steak smothered in onions, her favorite dish for guests. All my mother needed to create this culinary magic was an inexpensive cut of steak, an iron skillet, freshly sliced onions, salt, and pepper. As I entered the front room, Mama was waiting there, just as tall and shy as I remembered, and she hadn't aged a day. In fact, she had lost weight, which made her look even younger. We laughed and hugged each other as we sat on the old red couch and talked, with occasional interruptions as she went back to the kitchen to check on dinner.

Even though she spoke within the walls of her own house, her voice grew hushed when she told me about the Freedom Riders. Many of the young, idealistic whites from the East Coast lived with the colored people in their homes, ate with them, and went to their churches. "You know how young folk are; they got to have some free time, so some of them would go in the juke joints at night. And many of the white folk didn't like that at all. Eating, sleeping, and going to church with us were bad enough, but dancing with us they really didn't like!" There was apprehension in her voice as she told me these amazing things. So much was happening so fast, and this kind of socializing had not been part of our Mississippi world.

Except for occasional visiting in the fields, whites and blacks did not openly mix. The rules were strict, and as I listened to Mama, I knew that repercussions were to be expected.

In the midst of introducing me to aspects of the civil rights movement that hadn't made the evening news back in D.C., Mama suddenly started talking about Sargent Shriver and the Office of Economic Opportunity. I knew she had not met him, but she spoke his name with such familiarity that I laughed. Only a year before, Mama had been working as a maid, and now she knew more about the bureaucrats of Washington than I did.

The small living room was hardly big enough to contain the pride I saw in my mother's face as she spoke about going back to school, Head Start, and the impact the program was having on entire communities. I would not be able to visit all the communities of which she spoke, but I would see firsthand the changes taking place in my hometown. In the midst of the political buzz, there was a new surge of self-importance. The people working in the program had always worked hard, and now many of them were being paid well. For the first time, some of them had check stubs to analyze, taxes to be deducted, and Social Security to be paid. Their pride could not be denied.

Hearing about this life-changing program made me wish that I could bus the entire Congress in to see what political, economic, and social freedom could do for a people. Too many congressmen were arguing over the need for such a program and its cost, and were actually debating the value of lifting a people up. Some called Head Start a dole, a handout, overlooking the years of farm subsidies that our white counterparts had received. They kept using funding for Vietnam as an excuse, but Spike Ayers didn't buy it. He had convinced the people of our small town that our Delta home was just as important as that other delta across the sea. As a result, our whole town had become energized, and right in the midst of the change were my mother and Spike, who had fearlessly plugged our cause in Washington.

Some of the people who led the voter registration movement, like Rev. George Stovall from Greenville, were also involved. In fact, Head Start appeared to have grown out of those other civil rights efforts. I had earlier thought that the Office of Economic Opportunity had created Head Start, but my mother said no. According to her, the idea for Head Start was born in Greenville, right in the heart of the Delta.

This was a version of the story I had never heard. Just as Mama started telling it, she disappeared into the kitchen to finish preparing the evening meal. I wanted her to leave the cooking alone, but I had little choice but to count flowers on the wallpaper, which she had when I was a child, and wait while she stirred the gravy and made Kool-Aid, which she preferred to coffee. Finally, as I watched her through the French door that led to the kitchen, the only hint of elegance in an otherwise plain house, I saw her take off the apron and fold it over her arm, which meant that the food was nearly ready and we could continue our talk.

And talk we did, late into the evening. As we ate, she told me about her cousin, Dr. Matthew Page of Greenville, whom I had never met. The concept for Head Start, she said, had grown out of late-night discussions led by Dr. Page, Spike Ayers, and Bud Hall in Greenville at the Herbert Lee Community Center and at the Miller Memorial Center on Nelson and Broadway, a place in the black business district where civil rights people often met.

After the Student Nonviolent Coordinating Committee (SNCC), the Congress of Racial Equality (CORE), the National Association for the Advancement of Colored People (NAACP), the Delta Ministry, and others had worked together to ensure colored people's right to vote, they had found themselves faced with the problem of the plantation children. The plantations had grown up around the cotton industry and were maintained by a tenant farm system that evolved after the end of slavery. The work was hard, often demeaning, the pay was low, and the children of the farm workers suffered all the rigors of deep poverty.

"Something had to be done," she said, leaning toward me and laying her hand on my arm. "The voting rights workers saw little black children still eating with their hands and not potty trained. Their bodies showed lack of food." Just as I had been haunted by the bewildered faces and scrawny bodies of Vietnamese children I had seen on the nightly news, the civil rights workers here at home had been moved by the hollow eyes and poorly nourished bodies of plantation children who, faced with a stranger, would run like a jackrabbit shot from a gun. Thelma Barnes and Bernadine Young, both educators, were in the late-night discussion group that tried to come up with a way to improve these children's futures, and everyone finally settled on a grass-roots effort to prepare the children for preschool, which they called Head Start.

Initially, the local school districts and the state of Mississippi didn't want anything to do with it. Folks in Greenville like Charles Moore, Dr. Page, and Thelma Barnes persisted, with the help of others, like Andy Devine, Owen Brooks, and Harry Bowie of the Delta Ministry Foundation. They found a way to plead their cause to Lady Bird Johnson, and it was she who got the point over to the president and eventually to Sargent Shriver at the OEO. They found ways to circumvent the state's ability to block their funding. The Child Development Group of Mississippi (CDGM) received money for them from private funding sources that lay beyond the governor's reach but not beyond the reach of the people. They also had to get funding from Washington that could not be controlled by those local whites who not only did not share their dream but also felt that it threatened their way of life. "We needed all the help we could get," my mother said, "and when we eventually received some pilot money through CDGM, Head Start began."

With the centers, Mama said, a whole new industry opened up almost overnight. For the first time, educational opportunities were being brought to the children of Mississippi poor with the community heavily involved. Although funding remained a challenge, the program's acceptance as part of OEO insured its survival as one of the Great Society's shining stars. Operating outside the state's control, it kept quality education as its focus.

Even though the program was designed for all children, most of those it reached were colored. "The first centers started out in the churches," Mama pointed out, "but as more money came in, buildings were rented and trailers were purchased. Just think, if it had not been for getting people out to vote and all, the doors to the needs of the children might have stayed closed forever!"

I was delighted for my mother, not just because I loved her but also because I sensed her pride in herself and her role in swinging those doors open. She had always been smart, I knew, because as a child I had gone with her to the small plantation school where she taught. Even though she taught children of every age in an underfunded, over-looked church school that sat at the edge of a field, she used her ingenuity and drive to create visions of excellence. However, after she had taught there for a while, her personal dreams began to fade, and her life became like that of many of her friends and family.

For a number of years, it was almost as though Mama had entered a personal dark ages. It was a period when the man to whom she was married did not support the dreams, ambitions, and gifts she had that had been nurtured in the big house of her grandparents. As her self-confidence waned, she had returned to the fields and to the kitchens of white plantation owners to work as a maid. And, like scores of other American black women, she had resigned herself to that kind of life—a life, however, that she was determined her children would transcend.

When it was time for Claudette, my younger sister, to go to college, Mama had few options, so she grabbed the one that was available. She borrowed my sister's tuition from a white attorney in Greenville, Mr. Holland O. Felts, at an interest rate she could hardly afford. Mama had faith in her children, and we had faith in her. She had seen the pattern—Poppa had also been determined that she would go to college, and he and Mama Pearl worked to that end. For a while, their dreams for my mother looked as if they were coming true, but when Mama ventured north to Rust College, many miles from the shelter of her family's care, she grew homesick, dropped out, and came home.

Even though she returned to Glen Allan and the life she knew, Poppa's dream for her did not die. Early in her childhood, she had been made to feel special and was always surrounded by conversations that focused on their plans for her. My great-grandparents had planted good seeds, and while I had been away pursuing my dreams of living up north, she was becoming part of the new South. My mother's personal growth during the civil rights movement would have a profound effect on all of her children and on many other people who crossed her path.

My ability to comprehend data processing, which I had taken to be a great accomplishment, paled as I listened to this woman who had picked up her lost dreams and fashioned a new life, one worthy of her gifts. I knew it had not been easy. There were many people vying for the position for which she was eventually chosen. But she did it. Even though her earlier letters had hinted at her fear, Mother's smartness had not been lost in the cotton fields of the Delta or washed away in the kitchens of the wealthy. To secure her job, she had returned to school, this time the University of Alabama, where she had excelled, and to her own surprise she had become a model center director in the Mississippi Head Start program. Poppa had been right all along.

In just a short time, Yates Center gained national recognition because of the response it elicited from parents and their children. And the news of my mother's success reached Jackson, where Marian Wright Edelman was at work. Ms. Edelman took a deep interest in the children of the South and was instrumental in bringing then–Attorney General Robert Kennedy to the Delta. Yates Center was on the agenda as one of the places for Kennedy and other dignitaries to visit. I was so proud of my mother! She, her teachers, and their aides had invested their duties with love, and it was paying off. The children may have been physically and materially poor, but Yates Center, like many other Head Start centers, was unearthing treasures that others had overlooked.

On Monday, after spending my first weekend home visiting friends and family, as Ma Ponk had instructed me, I paid my visit to Yates Center, which was close to Greenville. On our way there, Mama told me how hard she had worked and prayed for her position as director. I smiled as I listened, knowing that if our Poppa were alive, he'd be awfully proud of his girl.

As we drove along the black-topped road, a white-washed building and a collection of small houses came into view, banded together at the edge of a large field. The center wasn't big, but the grounds were impressively clean. The long dirt sidewalk to the front door was lined with old tractor tires that had been cut in half and painted white, in bright contrast to the rich, green, wild Bermuda grass. I followed my mother as she unlocked the door for those who were already waiting, and soon I heard the laughter and the squeals of children as they were being unloaded from cars and vans. They were eager to be there, and the staff was eager to have them.

Before Head Start, many of these kids had been secluded in the back fields or had lived in homes where their future prospects were bleak. The civil rights movement in the Delta had started as an effort to register adults to vote, but it had led straight to the needs of the children, which was appropriate. After all, the movement was being fought for a better future for them.

As I stood to one side and watched, I saw that the center was a welcoming place to the children, as were the teachers and the aides who worked with them. Even though the center's legitimacy was being debated and its funding was uncertain, the little black faces, all scrubbed, greased, and sparkling, reflected none of this. In their innocence, unaware of the controversy that had created their world of hope, they just laughed, ate, and learned within these walls where they were being loved.

Soon after settling in, my mother and I went into her small office, where we had a conversation that I'll never forget. Even though I was an adult as well as a soldier, I felt like a child getting the advice of a lifetime, and I remained quiet as she made this little speech: "Cliff, it's so easy to close your heart to the parents that at first appear not to care about you or their children. You invite them to the center, but they won't come. And they really don't expect you to come to their house. But they were the children's parents, and I wanted to touch that paternal and maternal pride that was there. If the children were to be successful, the parents had to be part of the program. So, I decided to take it upon myself to visit them at their place and pull that pride out. When I'd get there, they seemed to want to just stand in the door and listen, but I had to get them to talk, so I invited myself in, asked for a drink of water, and just started talking.

"At first, I'd just comment on whatever I thought they were doing. If they were watching television, I wouldn't ask them to turn it off. I'd watch with them. Then I would look around to find something on a table or on their wall that we could use at the center and ask them if we could use it and if they could bring it over. Pretty soon, if the television was on, they'd get up and cut it off, and then we would talk. It wasn't my job to intimidate them, but to welcome them to help us educate their children. After a while, we'd laugh, talk, and make plans for the center. I didn't want any of our parents to ever think that they weren't important. You see, son, I knew how it felt to be overlooked and pushed back, and I wanted them up front and involved."

There was little I could say. I was moved by her sensitivity and skill in working with these families. Like Rosa Parks, I thought, she understood back seats and what it meant to be discounted and ignored. She was determined to use her position to generate goodwill among the community of parents, the children, and her staff. And I knew that she had.

Being at the center with my mother, her staff, and the children was the best reason to come home. I was never embarrassed that my mother had worked as a maid. It was just that I could never rid my mind of the earlier memory of her as a highly respected teacher. Now, I could once again see and hear the "Miss Mary" she had been, and I knew that the children she taught and the teachers she managed were receiving the best of care. I spent the entire day there. I ate lunch with them, and I played with the kids. It was a good day. I also visited the classes of Mary Jenkins and Irene Washington, two of Mother's close friends, and I spoke with Mrs. Zanders and Mrs. Perry, who were cooks and from the local area. They all seemed caught up in their roles within the movement, changing the lives of the children.

Over the week that followed, I made a hello and goodbye pilgrimage through Glen Allan that took me from Ma Ponk's house all the way uptown to visit Mrs. Knights, the older white lady at whose home I had worked on Saturdays. In addition to seeing Spike Ayers and the people who gathered to talk politics in his front yard, I went inside the juke joints, where I had never gone as a child. I had known Miss Albe and Phoebe, owners of two of the joints, all my life. If I wanted to catch most of the active group, I knew I'd find them there, either inside or parked on the roadside laughing and talking with each other. While standing with them on the well-traveled dirt road, I again saw their faith in the future. Just as Poppa and his preacher friends had found time to love and care and make community in spite of being relegated to an inferior social and economic place, these people lived with the fear of white reprisal. But that reality had always been there, and it never took away their ability to laugh. They had found good reasons to live, just as our grandparents before them. Even though their town, our home, was in the midst of the struggle, they found time to laugh and joke and welcome me home.

They were quick to talk with me about their war and service records. Most of the old men remembered World War II, and a few talked about Korea. They still spoke with pride about the boys who had gone off to serve and even spoke of me in the same fashion. I had left home. I had gone north. I had joined the service. That was good enough for them. Now, I was back, if only for a visit, walking their streets, shaking their hands, and telling them about the extreme cold in Maine and my classified assignment in Washington, D.C.

And, typical of the South, everyone spoke or at least waved from their pickup trucks. Somehow I knew that standing there on the roadside with them was the best thing to do. There were so many people to visit. There was so much to say, so much to see. I wanted to do it all. No one could be overlooked. My leave time was short, but Ma Ponk insisted that I make every stop or else she'd never hear the end of it. And so I went by to see Cousin Beauty and Cousin Savannah, and I sat on nearly every front porch in our small town. Everyone wanted me to taste a bit of food, a southern tradition that grows on you. I tried to accommodate each house. Full and festive when I was done, I had now made Ma Ponk happy. She could proudly walk uptown knowing that everyone that mattered to her would be saying, "Ponk sho raised that boy good. You know he came by to see me and ate a slice of caramel cake. Ain't forgot his upbringing."

I did not forget my upbringing, nor would I forget them. I would return to Washington full of new thoughts about my people, their struggle and their pride. I would remember their commitment to the children. And I would never forget how the movement was giving my mother a second chance.

FIVE

Just a Uniform Away

When I was a boy, good news never came at night. Over the years, the early morning darkness would be broken by a cry, "Ma Ponk, Ma Ponk, wake up, it's me, Johnny!" By the time I stumbled out of bed, Ma Ponk would already be up. We knew that such loud knocking and yelling always meant something was wrong. Within seconds, Ma Ponk would unlatch the deadbolt and open the screen door.

"They done put Sammy in jail again," a voice would come through the door.

"Lawd have mercy," Ma Ponk would answer, letting

Johnny, her nephew, in. "You set here. Lemme git myself to gather. I got to git this boy ready, too."

Ma Ponk never had to search for clothes. They always seemed to be right where she needed them to be, and I knew to get dressed. I knew we were going to go to town, and I watched as Ma Ponk reached under the innersprings and pulled out a worn brown paper bag. She said she never had any money, but she always seemed to find some in a crisis. And on such nights she knew that she would need it. After making sure that the house was locked up tightly, we would walk as fast as we could around to Poppa's house.

The lights would all be on. Poppa would be up and dressed. Sometimes people would be standing there crying, while others silently wrapped their arms around themselves. Poppa would tell everyone what had happened, how Uncle Sammy, who had a drinking problem, had picked a fight with some white men. Of course we would never know the whole truth—like what the others might have done to stir Sammy up when he was drunk. After Poppa asked us to pray—we always prayed—he would hold out his hat as the elders pooled their money. Ma Ponk would fish her folded bills out of her coat pocket and add them to the rest.

As we piled into Poppa's old car, Ma Ponk would mutter that she hoped it would start. No one did much talking. Poppa would sometimes hum a hymn as we made our way out of Glen Allan and headed up Highway One to Greenville, going to do what we could to bring Sammy home. Poppa, Mama Pearl, Daddy Julius, and Ma Ponk never liked making this trip, but they always went. Even though Grandmother Rosie, Ma Ponk's sister, had been Uncle Sammy's mother, he belonged to all of them, and no matter how often he got into trouble, they felt they had no choice but to go.

The tall, forbidding jailhouse sat in the center of Greenville. It was a place we all dreaded, one that always brought tears to the eyes of those that I loved. They had spent many hours and nights traveling the highway to bail out relatives and friends who were often falsely accused. For years I was too young to understand the cold, silent stares of the white jailers, but I remember being held close while walking down the center of the concrete corridor so I would not stray too near the heavy cell doors.

I was never searched, but the old folks were, and it was this disregard for who they were that probably affected them most. With hands raised and faces tight, Poppa and all who had come from Glen Allan went through this routine. They never talked. They only listened. They followed orders. They knew what to do, having done it many times before.

The jail was a bad place. There was no life there, and sometimes people never came home but were sent on to Parchman, the Mississippi state penitentiary. The resounding clang of the heavy iron cell doors made me determined never to be sent to jail. Ma Ponk always held me tightly by the hand, as if I would fall captive if left to wander by myself, and I would press my face into the long wool coat she always wore—no matter the season—when she went into town. I knew she disliked going to the jail, but when asked, she always went and took me with her. Never smiling, never saying more than she had to, she and the others would follow the jailer down the hall. This was not a place for her family, but if her family were there, she'd find a way to make it to their cell. "You be all right," she would comfort and soothe. "We gonna git you outta here."

One night in January 1968, four months after I had returned to Washington from my leave at home, I was awakened by a call. It was my mother, frantically telling me that my sister Clara Gene had been arrested during a demonstration on the University of Mississippi campus, "Ole Miss," where she was in school. She had been jailed, along with other students. I was stunned. Since child-hood, the word "jail" had held for me a ring of finality, of iron doors that closed and never opened.

Just as I had vowed that I would never be put in jail, I had never expected to hear such news about Clara or any of my other siblings. After all, our elders had better lives in mind for us and had talked about college daily. The histori-cally black colleges were to be our schools. We knew them all. Ma Ponk's son, Sidney, and Spike Ayers had gone to Alcorn; my mother had attended Rust as an undergraduate and later Mississippi Valley and Tougaloo to become accredited to teach; still later my sister Claudette went to Mississippi Valley; and the name of Fisk University was always spoken with awe. But not Ole Miss. Back then our world was colored, and so were our schools, and not even the dramatic entrance of James Meredith into Ole Miss in 1962 could make me imagine going there.

Thus, Clara's going to Ole Miss had, for us, been different. When she entered, the school still smoldered with the hostilities aroused by Meredith's entrance five years before—an entrance that had left an indelible impression of riots, soldiers, and jailings upon my mind. But Clara and Joyce, our cousin who went with her, had become part of the changing South and were brave enough to represent our little colored community at a school that most of us had never seen. Their decision to enroll and their acceptance became the talk of the town. Just as others had carried the community's blessings north, Clara and Joyce would carry their blessings to Ole Miss. "Sho, they smart 'nough to go," the comments would come. "An *A* is an *A* no matters who's got it." "Yes sir," someone else would add, "dem girls been 'paring for this all da time. Miz Ross and 'fessor Moore 'pared them for it." Glen Allan's colored community was still pioneering, it was clear, and their children were still validating their dreams.

Even though we grew up in a "separate but equal" school environment, which meant that our schools were underfunded and ill-equipped, our families put us first. Though many of them had barely darkened the school's door, they were determined that we would reach the stars. Even in the fields, while cotton was being chopped and picked, they would talk across the rows about how higher education was the key to a good future. They loved calling the black male teachers "professor." And they were convinced that we all "had the goods" and that one day we would know it. Thus when Joyce and Clara no doubt surprised the white community with their acceptance to Ole Miss, it was no surprise to the colored folk. They knew the girls "had the goods."

Armed with academic scholarships, good grades, and courage, the girls headed to Oxford, Mississippi, the home of Ole Miss. Outwardly, my mother was proud, but inside she was fearful as she realized that her daughter was going to what was still an almost all white school. Determined to provide what help she could, Mama accepted the challenge, prayed for Clara's safety, and tried to make her feel secure. Mindful of this, I felt badly that I had not gone up to the university to visit Clara when I was home on leave. I was excited for her, but I was also aware that she had enrolled during a deeply unsettled time and that there were likely to be people who would look down on her, shut her out, and call her names.

While at home I had read an old newspaper account of how, during the time Meredith was trying to enroll, the Reverend Roy Grisham, the white pastor of the Oxford University Methodist Church, had stood up and called for change and reconciliation. Rev. Grisham's courage nourished my hope that a light was shining, that America would eventually find her way, and that Mississippi would eventually become part of the light that we would see. That news article reminded me that not all people turned their backs on doing right.

On the other hand, we should have been able to look to the church for leadership all along, but it appeared that the white church in particular had gone underground just when "light" was really needed. In 1962, right before Meredith officially entered the university, all kinds of traditional fears and biases were unleashed, and Oxford, the tranquil home of William Faulkner, became a place that the ugly and the profane claimed as their own. Because such people feared losing a world that had been built on racial separation, the campus became the Virgin of the South, whose "purity" must be protected at all costs.

While the cameras brought the troubles at Ole Miss to the attention of the world, Rev. Grisham was declaring from his pulpit that Mississippians, both black and white, were responsible for the fuel that had ignited the fire on his campus. He deplored the cowardice of the church while he was personally reaching out to shield students from racists who wanted to do them harm. Rev. Grisham's sermons and actions brought hope in a time of dim light, and the national media profiled the Sunday sermon he delivered on October 7, 1962. Some found it difficult to believe that a person like Grisham would dare to come to the forefront, call for calm, and plant seeds that would grow years later on the Ole Miss campus, but I felt that in some small way these actions would help my sister and her friends who had followed Meredith there.

Now, though, as I waited for a second call from my mother, I was left to imagine my sister's plight. Being hundreds of miles away didn't help. As I lay in my cell-like barracks room with its plain walls and two spartan cots, my imagination ran wild. Once again I walked down the corridor of the Greenville jail, seeing the old black hands clutching the bars, hearing my own heartbeat, which sounded louder than footsteps. Once again, not daring to look around, I was clinging to Ma Ponk's hand as we followed the white jailer into the depths of his world, where all I could hear over and over were these words: the prisoner, the prisoner, the prisoner. My uncle had a name, but not in jail. There, he was no longer Sammy, my Aunt Rosie's son; he was just the prisoner. Now my little sister was "the prisoner" as well.

I had not thought about Uncle Sammy and those trips to the Greenville jail in a long time, but Mother's call about Clara brought the memories back. And the old fears now surfaced in a way they had never done when I had heard reports of civil rights workers being jailed. Those had been people I respected and admired but did not personally know. They were soldiers in a domestic offensive being fought on my behalf. Clara's incident gave the movement a face and name that I knew well, that were indeed a part of me.

There was no news about the girls, who had been hauled off to the Lafayette County jail, but we did know that the young men who had taken part in the demonstration had been sent to Parchman. They had to have been scared, many of them just young black men straight from the plantation. I anguished for the parents of the boys who were taken there. Parchman was no place for them.

As I continued to wait in the all but empty barracks for my mother's second call, there were no sounds, no laughter, no arguments to divert me; all was quiet except for the ongoing conversations in my head. Uncle Sammy's sad face wouldn't go away; nor would the fear I felt for Clara, which was accompanied by the recollected sound of clanging iron doors.

The call finally came that gave me peace. Although it had seemed like forever, Clara was released from jail, unharmed, by the end of the first day. Beyond that, my mother told me little. She was just happy that her daughter was safe. It would be years before I would learn from Clara herself everything that had happened—years after she had graduated, worked as an accountant in Japan, and had come home to marry and start her own family.

Two decades later, seated at the dining room table in my house in Tulsa, she finally told us what had happened to her and what life was like for pioneering black students at Ole Miss. "We were all nicely dressed," she said, "our faces were scrubbed, and we were motivated to succeed, but we lived with a constant fear that became our shadow. As we walked silently by, white students usually gathered in groups. 'Monkeys, go back to Africa!' they would cry. That's what they thought of us. They thought so little!"

"But what about the arrest?" I asked.

"Oh yes. The arrest. We had done nothing wrong!" Clara exclaimed. "We had gone to an Up with People concert on the campus that had been the object of protest by some of the black students, but my friends and I had not taken part. Nevertheless, we were the right color, and a few white students lied and signed false testimonies that placed us at the protest. As a result, about fifteen of us were hauled off to jail like common criminals!"

As Clara talked about the trip to jail, her demeanor darkened. "Even though we were afraid, we tried to be bold and not show it. The processing, though rude, was not of much consequence, but when they led us to the cell and I heard the sound of doors being shut, I knew I was in trouble. My first few moments behind those iron bars were like a lifetime of freedom lost."

"Clara, how did you get the word out that you were in trouble and needed help?" I asked. "What about your dean of women, Catherine Ray? Did she help? You always spoke kindly of her as a kind of oasis in your desert."

"Dean Ray was a good woman. She went beyond expectations to ensure that the black girls had 'little extras' like snacks and spending money. And even though she was white, she helped make our lives bearable. But this was different. We were in 'black folk' trouble, and I didn't need a hair net or money to go home. I needed out of jail. And I thought of the one person who loved us at every turn, an older black lady, Mrs. Bryant." Clara brightened as she brought her hands to her face, "Yes, it was Mrs. Bryant."

"Who was she?" I asked.

"She lived in Oxford. Her home was our home," said Clara, "our place to go on the weekends. We became her daughters. She watched out for us like we were kin. She didn't have much, but she shared all she had."

When our cousin Joyce, who hadn't been with Clara and the others at the concert, found out that Clara had been jailed, she immediately called home for prayer and support and then went straight to Mrs. Bryant, who responded quickly.

"Mrs. Bryant called the charges 'trumped up,'" said Clara, "and of course she was right. She prayed that they'd set a reasonable bail. Then, armed with nothing more than Joyce's story, she made her way through the black community, rounding up the caring people who would be willing to put up their homes and property as collateral if needed to secure our release. Yes, it was Mrs. Bryant, one lady I will always remember."

Although many years had passed, our conversation brought the reality of both love and hate to my dining room table, along with the complexities of the Mississippi that had been our home. There had been good whites, and there had been racists. And there had been those black people like Mrs. Bryant who had just been waiting for a reason to stand up full measure. However, the jeers and taunts kept ringing in my head as if they had happened only the day before. The wounding cry "Monkeys, go back to Africa" had been a jeer not at a person I didn't know but at a girl who was part of me. And even though I had been in the air force in Washington, D.C., the insults that were yelled at my sister and her friends had included me. They had been insulting me, their soldier, when they yelled, "Monkeys, go back to Africa." Clara's arrest had made me realize that I was just a uniform away from the taunts, jeers, and sneers of those who didn't care to know me or discover my life, a life that I was trying to make full.

I stayed in the military and Clara lived through her personal trauma, which could have been much worse. The embers for a real fire were there. The hostility needed to fan the coals was there, but there was also a gentle rain that kept the fires down, a rain of words from those with level heads, including Dean Ray. For many, James Meredith's attendance at Ole Miss had been a misguided violation of their way of life. Even though his admission brought out the selfishly proud and the openly profane, there in the midst of those loud voices were a few that called for reason and calm, and for the church to come out of hiding.

With Clara out of jail and safe, I was able again to focus on my job and the classes I was taking at the University of Maryland. I was determined not to let this act of cowardly racism keep me from obtaining the goals I had established. Although I could do nothing to change my color or make people appreciate me, I still had within me the power to make my grandpa proud by earning college credits and doing the job expected at the Eighty-ninth.

However, my sister's brief arrest had also personalized the movement for me in a special way, and I began to accept and discuss these feelings with some of my closer friends. Just as the uniform had made me a Vietnam soldier by association, so had my sister's arrest made me a participant in the struggle for civil rights and made me yearn for a way to leave the turn-road where I had watched in safety. It was the uniform and all it stood for that had kept me there. I realized now more than ever that the struggle for freedom would exact a price, and not just from admired, respected strangers but from people like me. I could hear voices calling, and even if I wasn't sure what I would do, I was bound to answer.

Robert Francis Kennedy
Senator of the United States
November 20, 1925 - June 6, 1968

SIX

Politics:

"White Folks' Business Ain't Ours"

Although I had now begun to seek them, there were few opportunities for active political engagement available to a military man. But then, for most of my life, political engagement was not something I had sought. In Poppa's house, politics was a subject cautiously discussed, usually at night behind closed doors. Thus, it was all the more remarkable to me when I was home on leave to see the giant leap into political action that the people in my town had made.

When I was small, my first awareness of politics had

come one Saturday afternoon when I was on my way to Peru Plantation to visit my mother's cousins, Lula and Buster. As we drove through Glen Allan's small business district, past Mr. Jake Stein's dry goods and grocery store, I saw a big poster of a white man, just his head, that seemed to cover the outside wall of the store. It was a poster of Democratic presidential candidate Adlai Stevenson, who was on his way to defeat by Dwight Eisenhower. When I asked my mother who it was, she simply said, "That's white folks' business; ain't ours."

My only other brush with politics came when I was slightly older. Funds were being raised by the community to send along with Deacon Joe Maxey to an NAACP meeting in Baltimore. "Those peckerwoods don't like this one bit," said Ma Ponk, but despite her fears, she decided to take me with her to a special meeting at St. Mark's Missionary Baptist Church. Ma Ponk always spoke kindly of all people, even those who disregarded her age, wisdom, and strength, but she used "peckerwoods" to describe those whites who seemed to gain power and take pleasure from belittling black people's lives. Nevertheless, her customary courage overcame her obvious apprehension, and we locked the house and quietly walked down the road to the church.

By the time we got there, the special service had already begun, so we quickly found a seat near the back, instead of near the "Mothers' Board" where Ma Ponk always sat. The fundraising had started, and I watched as it was done very quietly and under close guard. After the money was collected and a special hymn was sung, Daddy Julius and old Preacher Hurn laid on hands and prayed for Deacon Maxey's safety. As Ma Ponk, Aunt May Ann, and I walked silently home along the gravel road, Ma Ponk whispered her own quick prayer, "Keep 'im, Lawd," and squeezed my hand.

Until I went home on leave to Glen Allan in September 1967, politics had remained "white folks' business" for me. But on that journey, I witnessed the changes I had read about and seen on television and saw people who were making them happen. A young black student from Jackson State University, Alvin Chambliss, had been inspired by Spike Ayers, by a Jackson State political science professor, Dr. Calvin Miller, and by Fannie Lou Hamer, the share-cropper who, once having stood up, determined never to bow again. Alvin had come to Glen Allan to soak up Spike's wisdom and to learn from Mrs. Hamer how to work at the grass-roots level. Spike and Fannie Lou were for the little folk, and they never seemed to waver. All of this crowded into my mind as I tried to return to the safe, predictable world I had left behind. Mama had been wrong years before when she said politics was not our business. It was, and somehow it had to be mine.

For the people back home, Spike Ayers had become the lead man, a role he would continue to fulfill until his death, almost twenty years later, in 1986. I knew the value of lead men, having seen them set the pace and standards in the fields most of my life. The lead man always got to the fields early, selected the first row, and set the momentum for the day. Spike had done this for the people of Glen Allan. The movement was their field, and he had led them into the harvest and challenged me.

Just as Spike and the others kept me focused and mindful of activities back home, Dr. Martin Luther King Jr. had become the lead man for the nation. He had roused America's conscience in the early morning of the movement and had set the pace for a people that he had brought to the fields in time. And now, with a more committed heart, I heard his message more clearly than ever before.

Although Dr. King had become a national figure several years before, I had not heard much about him while living in Glen Allan. He had already sent his heart to the nation from the Birmingham jail, but to many of us back then, he was known simply as the young preacher over in Alabama. It was not until I was living in St. Louis that I first became mesmerized by his ability to speak and hold the attention of the world. At age seventeen, I found a pew between the sacks of sweet potatoes and the pile of watermelons in Uncle Madison's confectionery, my eyes fastened on the small black and white television that hung from the ceiling. I and the other people in the store who sat glued to the screen joined the multitude that had gathered at the base of the Lincoln Memorial in Washington, D.C. No one moved. We were all transfixed as Dr. King reached out and touched our hearts, daring us to dream with him. For days afterward, I heard his voice, and the promise of his dream was renewed for me years later after my visit home. I knew then that I was witnessing a harvest, a harvest of brotherhood.

Now, back at Andrews, I didn't know what I could do or what would be acceptable for me to do as a soldier, but I was determined to find out. As I searched for a way to join, I was aware that Dr. King was also being challenged. A steadily rising corps of young activists were saying that the urban movement had left him behind, that his methods were too passive and would not work in the North. New voices and new leaders emerged, fiery voices like Stokely Carmichael, who used phrases we had previously uttered only in secret. Carmichael, with his thin frame and over-sized Afro, issued a call for black power, which became a rallying cry for the colored youth of urban America.

These young people had not marched in Selma or faced the dogs in Montgomery, yet they sought to muscle in to the front of the field. Dr. King had marched right into our hearts and had given voice to our souls. Yet while he had mainly focused on the segregated South, our northern cousins had become increasingly vocal in their demands for acceptance into the American mainstream.

These were people whom I had once dreamed were productive and free, which was one reason I had wanted to move north. But they had problems, too—inadequate housing, low-paying jobs, and discrimination. And their leaders—Carmichael, Huey Newton, and H. Rap Brown—

burned with a retributive fire and claimed rights of leadership that I personally felt were yet to be earned. No wonder, then, that among many people in the North, the black Muslims held great appeal. The Muslims were vocal, unapologetic, and displayed an aggressiveness contrary to the practices of Dr. King. While Dr. King sought to join hands, they were pointing out that white America's hands held guns. From their temples the word went out that Vietnam was a white man's war in which our young black men were being sacrificed.

Nonetheless, Dr. King persisted in developing a broader agenda, one that would include help for the urban poor as well as a voice against the war. His criticism of the war sent a great stir throughout the country, which I felt in the Eighty-ninth. Before, Dr. King had been quietly accepted by some, tolerated by many, and considered dangerous by others. Now, his perspectives on the war caused heated conversations in my office, where he was seen to have overstepped the bounds of his legitimate concerns.

Although mingled voices of many groups now filled the air, all clamoring for volunteers to join them to bring about an end to injustice, Dr. King's voice was still the most compelling to me as he urged us not to forget America's poor. There were millions of Americans of all races, he said, who had not eaten even the crumbs from the table of plenty, and we were to make room at our table for them.

King then began to make bold plans to bring the poor of America to the nation's capital. Many projected a repeat performance of the massive march on Washington of 1963. Even though some of his top lieutenants—Jesse Jackson, James Bevel, and Bayard Rustin—did not completely agree, King was determined, and I was glad. Finally, I would have a chance to begin to do my part. Because I was stationed at Andrews, I would be able to join this second great Washington march.

As the needy of the nation caught wind of Dr. King's broadened agenda, he was overwhelmed with requests by those seeking justice to plead their case, and he tried to accommodate as many as he could. This commitment took him to Memphis in early April 1968 in support of the sanitation workers who were striking for higher wages and better working conditions. Still trying to show the long-range value of nonviolence, he met with the young and angry of Memphis to try to dissuade them from violence, which he felt could become an agenda all its own.

While he spoke in Memphis, I was mentally preparing for the Poor People's Campaign, an effort by the members of the Southern Christian Leadership Conference to create within the city of Washington, D.C., a living reminder of the plight of America's poor. The SCLC had been started by Dr. King and the Reverend Ralph Abernathy to galvanize and organize the obvious leadership within the black churches. This leadership was of extreme importance to the expanding civil rights movement. For the gathering, fifteen acres of sight-seeing meadowland, strategically located between the Lincoln Memorial and the Washington

Monument, were chosen to become squatters' territory that would house the representatives of our nation's poor. They were all expected to come, the black and poor, the Indian and poor, the Mexican and poor, and the Appalachian white and poor. For once, I would be in the fields where the crops were.

My excitement was short-lived. The morning after Dr. King spoke in Memphis, the barracks halls were filled with urgent voices. I heard words like "shot," "murdered," and "assassinated." As I walked into the john where the guys were talking, no name was mentioned. They all knew, and they thought that I knew, but I didn't.

When they gave me the news that King had been killed, news that I had miraculously missed the night before, my world seemed to shatter. I was suddenly scared, and I felt conspicuously "colored." I cried and cried, and when I stopped, I found it difficult to talk. I had believed King to be invincible. He had won the Nobel Peace Prize. He had taught us to fight the invading demon of racism together. And it was his voice that had kept our hands clasped. With no one to galvanize us, what would we do? Dr. King, a voice of reason and hope, was gone. He had challenged us as a nation. I had wanted to be a part of his continued efforts in Washington. Now he was dead, shot while trying to help America be good.

I had to go to the office. It was supposed to be a regular work day, but Andrews was on alert. Rumors of riots flew, and I felt that all black soldiers were being watched, although the few that I encountered were simply shocked and numb like me. All day long I fearfully watched the news. Mourning overtook the base, and King was on everyone's tongue.

Appropriately for a lead man who was among the first in the field, Dr. King's body was borne in a simple casket pulled by mules through the streets of Atlanta, the city of his birth. But as the reality of his loss gave way to hurt, anger, and fear, many of his mourners took to the streets, sending smoke signals around the world. Thousands became foot soldiers, not to march nonviolently in his memory but to riot as distraught souls who sought solace by lashing out.

For days afterward the tension in my office was profound. We didn't know what to say to each other. How could Dr. King be venerated when, only weeks earlier, his voice against the war had been denounced? Our color held us captive. Suddenly it was as though Sgt. Myrick and I stood for Dr. King and all black people. Everyone's condolences over his death were offered to us. Likewise, as though the others collectively bore the guilt of his white assassin, James Earl Ray, we accepted their apologies. It would be days before the tensions eased and some of us gained enough courage to talk about the tragedy of Dr. King's death and the gravity of America's loss. When finally we did, we wrestled with the question of how we had gotten so entangled in this web of historical hates and fears.

As we made our way through the month of April, I was drawn into friendship with three airmen who had brought an active awareness of political issues into the military with them. For them, discussing politics was a part of life's routine. Howard and Hugh Johnson, fraternal twins from Battle Creek, Michigan, and their friend Angelo, from a beach town in California, became my steady companions as outward events pressed us to redefine our personal roles and purposes. Perhaps we fancied ourselves intellectuals; we had begun to discuss the quality of our participation in society, much as our peers were doing on campuses throughout America. Together we questioned our reason for living and wondered how our lives could have value if we were not politically and socially involved. We were not only soldiers, after all, but young men with feelings.

Beneath our uniforms, the four of us had a growing passion and a genuine zeal to do our small part to make a difference in our world. In the 1960s, thanks to John F. Kennedy, there was a pervasive feeling that individuals could truly make a difference. And I had been challenged much earlier by the porch people of the Mississippi Delta. They too believed that the individual could make a difference, as they clung to the belief that tomorrow was always the brightest day.

Although I knew very little about campaigns, elections, and grassroots involvement, my three friends seemed to be experts in politics. They had all come from homes where political activity was a way of life. But it was not until I was at home on leave that first time that I saw the colored people of Glen Allan participating in national politics. Robert Clark had become the first black congressman elected in the state of Mississippi since Reconstruction, and growing in Glen Allan and like communities were the political beginnings for a new party to be formed within our state, the Mississippi Freedom Democratic Party, which would embrace Fannie Lee Hamer as their leader and emblematic soul.

Together my friends and I dreamed that Robert Kennedy would run for president. Like most young people, we were all still mesmerized by John Kennedy's presidency. Now we looked to Robert to become our lead man. Although he had declared he wouldn't run, we watched and listened as he moved further and further from the policies of the Johnson administration, increasingly speaking out against the war. As attorney general during his brother's administration, he had also gone south to the Delta and was given credit for assisting in the nationalization of Project Head Start, although I learned many years later that it had been his mother, Rose Kennedy, and her interest in children that really spurred his actions. I would have to learn about politics and presidential campaigns, but I would not have to learn how to become committed. All I needed was a lead man to choose the first row and set the pace. I was ready, as were my friends.

Since we all knew that our military status would limit our involvement, we charged Angelo with the task of finding out what we could and could not do. We wanted to be in place and ready for action if RFK ran. For the first time in my life, I found myself following primaries. We watched the New Hampshire primary with great interest as Senator Eugene McCarthy nearly upset President Johnson. Even though Robert Kennedy had declared he wasn't going to run for the presidency, he had been making overtures to the various coalitions of southern liberals. "Overtures" was a new word to me, but Howard and Hugh understood and said that something big was in the air.

On March 16, 1968, just a month before the assassination of Dr. King, Robert Francis Kennedy announced his candidacy for president of the United States. The four of us were overjoyed. We had already decided to become involved at a small level in his campaign, and Angelo had found out that we could volunteer as part of the boiler room activity during our off-duty time. Within days, I found myself moving from a few youthful political memories to the possibility of helping to elect the next president.

Kennedy was popular among the workers of America, blacks, other minorities, and many of the poor, and he brought new strength to the antiwar crusade. Although I was delighted with his announcement, many of my youthful counterparts were not. They had rallied behind McCarthy and were calling my lead man "Bobby come lately." With President Johnson's decision not to run, it had become politically easier for Robert Kennedy to do so.

It didn't bother me that Sgt. Myrick and I were the only people in our office supporting Kennedy. After witnessing the courage of my friends back home, it had become much easier for me to stand up for my beliefs. Many of the men in the Eighty-ninth felt more comfortable with the Republican candidate, Richard Nixon. The war had become very divisive for us. On one hand, we all wanted it to end, but we also had to confront the country's apparent flight from those who had already died. Had their deaths been in vain? As a soldier, I never publicly criticized the war, but I wanted it to end. I had friends in Vietnam that I wanted to see come home, including my best friend from the service, Paul Demuniz. For many, Nixon was the man who would bring honor to those dead and bring the others home.

When the Kennedy people finally announced the location of his campaign headquarters, I called to make an appointment for my friends and myself. Being soldiers from the Eighty-ninth Presidential Wing was not a bad calling card for volunteers. It got us through. A few days after I called, the four of us would go down to meet the campaign coordinator and determine what we could do and when.

As the day drew closer, I became apprehensive. My color had kept me separated from southern politics all my life, and now I feared that again, in spite of what I wanted, this could turn out to be white people's business and not mine. These were issues that my friends did not have to think about. Being white, they had perceived involvement in politics as their right and responsibility. On the other hand, I knew that if this worked out, my volunteer effort, however limited, would have me crossing lines and laboring in fields that I had previously watched from afar. I also knew that the military, where I had encountered more integration than I had ever known, had actually prepared me for this challenge. Despite some racism in the service, there was a concerted effort to mold all airmen and soldiers into a single unit, making it necessary for us to leave many of our traditional fears and biases outside the gate. The Kennedy campaign headquarters was outside the base, and I wondered if I would be welcomed there as well.

Not wanting these worries to become an issue, I didn't share them with my friends. I wanted to believe that RFK's campaign and those in charge would be inclusive in their planning. When the day for our appointment came, we all went into the District armed with our enthusiasm and idealism. It would be all right, I kept telling myself. It had to be all right. We were there early. We were excited. We could not wait to be part of the activity we saw and the energy we felt. Posters of Kennedy's face were everywhere, peering from every window, looming over water fountains, and looking down every hall.

While we waited, I thought about Poppa. I knew that he

would be proud of me. In a small way, I was now doing what he and many of his friends could only dream about. Also, although I was never his close friend, I wanted Spike Ayers back in Glen Allan to know that I was trying to cross the line and join with them. Although Spike had never verbally challenged me to find a niche in the social revolution to which he was committed, I was challenged nonetheless by what I saw him doing. And now I found it exciting just sitting in the midst of the hopeful campaign workers. There were young people everywhere. Campaign literature was stacked along every wall. Telephones rang nonstop.

We didn't talk much because we were so awed by all the people moving in and out. When we were finally summoned, we tried to look like college men as we followed a striking woman in her thirties to the area where the volunteers were screened, briefed, and assigned. Although taken with our political possibilities, we were also taken with the volunteer coordinator. Tailored, poised, and direct, she reminded us of the handsome Mrs. Robinson from the movie *The Graduate*, and we hung on her every word.

She was aware of the constraints on our time and had flagged some possibilities that wouldn't conflict with the military. We didn't care what they were. We just wanted to be there. I was prepared to stuff envelopes, empty the trash, and put up signs. We performed many different tasks, and I even appeared in a pack scene of young people for Kennedy that was featured in *Look* magazine. The volunteer work was so absorbing that we planned to work up until the last possible day before the November election.

During this time, I met Kennedy's wife, Ethel, and their two older boys, and I was told I would get to meet Kennedy himself at a Georgetown volunteer party, where we were to gather in early June to celebrate the results of the California primary, which he was expected to win. In the meantime, all of us focused upon our work, and I felt as if I were a part of history. For us the future was growing brighter, and we were all playing our part.

Although we basked in the promise of our candidate, many people in cities across America were not so joyful. Nearly one hundred cities had been torn by riots and hundreds of people in this domestic offensive had died. We felt more than ever that we needed Kennedy's voice and leadership to bring about peace and calm. As we continued to work to bring that victory about, we kept our eyes on California.

On June 6, 1968, only three months after having announced, Robert Kennedy won the California presidential primary. When he spoke before his enthusiastic crowd of supporters in the ballroom at the Ambassador Hotel in Los Angeles, I knew that I had made the right choice. He told the crowd that the violence, the disenchantment with our society, the divisions between races, between the poor and the more affluent, between age groups, and the divisions over the war in Vietnam could be overcome. That was all I wanted to hear. And to think I was working on his campaign! But with his speech of victory over, Robert Kennedy left the ballroom and our lives. Twenty-five hours after Sirhan Sirhan emerged from the crowd and shot Kennedy in the head, another lead man died.

From the time he was shot until he died, I watched television every moment I could. "No way can this be happening!" I kept saying, over and over. "No way!" Robert Kennedy was going to come back to Washington and we would all be going to the victory party in Georgetown. He would come back and I would continue to pursue my dream of helping bring about a political victory that I was confident could change the world. But when it was confirmed that he had died, I fled to my room, where I threw a chair against the wall and then, cursing and crying, threw another.

I realized anew that even though the military was showing me a more integrated way of life and was giving me important new work experiences, I was still black. The legacy of slavery and the burden of my color were still there. And I had come from the world of the South—a world where advocates were needed, where Poppa had served as a go-between with whites and blacks, where Deacon Joe Maxey had found the time to keep our small community connected to the NAACP, and where Spike Ayers still voiced our concerns for the children of the Delta. To some degree, the Kennedy brothers had become to me a family of advocacy, able to reach places that I could not reach and bring me pieces of America that I needed. I now felt bereft of help as my small barracks room reverberated with my anger and despair. Sleep eluded me and fear stood watch.

With John F. Kennedy dead, Martin Luther King murdered, and Robert Kennedy gone, I suddenly felt alone in a crowded world. The great hope I had placed in Kennedy's election was gone, and I didn't see anyone else moving up to take his place. The go-betweens were all being killed. I ached over this man's death. I wanted to stay cooped up in my room. I feared the stares of white people and conversations that might draw us into conflict, and for a while I mourned alone. As RFK's bright star sank into the night, so it seemed did all of our goals and efforts.

As I mourned, I remembered my childhood dreams. I knew that I was no longer the same young man who had left the South with a short list of simple goals. I had been swept up by the agony of the war and overwhelmed by the demands and expectations of the civil rights movement. I had gone home to visit, to be refreshed, to take my leave, and instead had been challenged to work in a field I could only watch from afar. Now, the tragedy of the assassinations had physically removed from me men who had demanded my best. Although their voices would remain with me, serving as guides for other times of harvest that were bound to come, for the moment I didn't know what to do or where to turn.

SEVEN

Adrift in D.C.

Voices of calm and reconciliation were few as the race to name a contender, a new lead man for the Democratic Party, heated up. I had lost all interest and so had my three friends. I never went to Hubert Humphrey's campaign office to offer my help. I sat back to watch. But I was not at ease.

I knew that Spike and those back home probably suffered more setbacks on a daily basis than I had encountered in all my life. They didn't quit. They moved on to the next day, the next opportunity, the next crop. Where did they get their strength? I had gotten courage from them. I had been challenged by what I saw. I had not acquired the will to keep moving when I felt there was nowhere else to go and nothing left to do, and so I began simply to look ahead to the day my enlistment would be up, August 18, 1968.

Some friends, sensing my mood, offered to help me drown my sorrows. I was tempted, but I had never learned to drink; that was a line I had not crossed. Of course I knew the people back home who drank, including the old folk who always kept their liquor in a brown paper bag. Over time the bag took on the shape of the bottle. We knew to pretend we didn't see it. And the juke joints of the Delta, where sorrows could be openly drowned and hurts forgotten, had been totally off-limits to me. Not that I didn't want to go, but Ma Ponk was determined that I never go inside. The only times I did, it was to get a good, greasy hamburger and cold soda water, nothing more. The juke joints were called the houses of worship for the devil, and liquor was the communion wine.

The buildings that housed the juke joints' mysterious life were old frame houses plastered with outdated, weather-worn posters of the blues greats who had in earlier years serenaded those who came to listen, dance, and forget their regulated life. The splendid Seeburg jukeboxes were there, with their colored lights, and I had secretly admired those "shrines of Satan" that, upon being fed a quarter, would belt out the blues as if the singers were right there in the room. When the machine lit up, the mechanical hand would gently find the right record and place it on the waiting altar—the turntable—and Ruth Brown's voice would brassily invade our hearts and minds. On my visit home, new sounds from Detroit, Motown, blasted out the juke joint doors. Still, it was the blues that held my attention while I stood for hours beside the door, talking with my friends.

As I counted my remaining days in the military, watched the presidential race, and listened to the rhetoric about ending the war, I spent increasing amounts of time at the King Street Assembly in Alexandria, Virginia. Although I never discussed the war or the issues that tugged at my heart with my friends at that church, it became a place where I could hide safely from my hurts. Being white, the King Street Assembly was very different from the churches I knew in the Delta. Most of the colored Delta churches were out front attacking racism, providing voting space, becoming temporary Head Start centers, and mobilizing all the community. Not so the churches in Alexandria. At the King Street Assembly, the soul was the focus and the enemy was hell. It was not a place where the headlines of the day became Sunday sermons, but I did meet Marguerite Becker there, who provided a refuge for me.

Marguerite, her two daughters, and a young man named Johnny, who rented a room from her, ran something like an at-home mission for soldiers. Marguerite had it all planned: Keep the soldiers busy, keep them in church, keep them at her house, and then send them back to the base—so there would be no time for downtown D.C. and drinking. It worked, and I must admit that those Sundays at her home were a welcome retreat where I could close out the hurt, forget the war, and just live. Marguerite was also a good cook, and this was my first time to sit at a dining room table with a group of nonmilitary white people and eat a meal, except for the times back home when I ate lunch with Mrs. Knights, a white lady for whom I worked.

Food, games, and discussions about dates filled our afternoons. Even though I participated, I felt that I was on the outside looking in. I was still quietly recovering, and I had no one to date. My friend Wally, who sometimes gave me rides back and forth to the University of Maryland campus in his white Triumph, had introduced me to the King Street Assembly, and he was dating. Wally's roommate, Bob, was engaged to Marguerite's niece. Johnny had been married, and I thought he had his eyes on one of Marguerite's daughters. But I had no one. There were girls my age but not my color. We never discussed that, either. Marguerite was somewhat a Pollyanna. She never brought up anything that would cause an argument. She just ignored it. We never discussed race or even the war. So on Sundays I lived in their world, and it took me a while to feel comfortable enough to stretch out and enjoy the run of the house like the others. I had friends of other races in the military, but this was different. This was social integration.

The issues of my heart were real but were never explored within our church group. We seemed to have valued each other's souls, but there was little or no conversation about our real-life issues. The church in Alexandria became a turn-road for me and so did Marguerite's table. I knew that feelings about race and the war existed, but they were never discussed. Likewise, all the demonstrations in the South that were tearing lives apart were never discussed, and no outright condemnation of racism and bigotry ever came forth. Maybe it was easier for all of us to live in two worlds and to keep our superficial one free of our biases, prejudice, and fear.

In spite of what we didn't discuss, Wally, Bob, and I enjoyed those Sunday afternoons. Marguerite's pot roast and potatoes welcomed us, and we could always go back for more. I don't know if I was her "mission field" or not, but without question she was becoming my missionary. Just like Ma Ponk, who believed that church matters should always come first, Marguerite was now, without knowing it, perpetuating all the prohibitions that Ma Ponk had taught me all my life.

As much as I enjoyed Marguerite's home, it never relieved me of my desire to do socially useful work. As my countdown to discharge continued, my desire to do something that I could say made a difference overwhelmed me.

But what? I couldn't go to Chicago to the Democratic Convention, and I had no more leave time. Since I would be in Washington until mid-August when my tour was up, I harbored a distant hope that something would come of the plan to implement the Poor People's Campaign. However, there was so much turmoil and controversy within the leadership of the Southern Christian Leadership Conference that I doubted they would ever reach an agreement in time for me to be involved.

In the tradition of the men in my family who had gone off to war, I had come to Washington with the full intention of dating and creating personal memories that would last a lifetime. My trip back home in September had rearranged most of my priorities. The friends I had left behind at Dow had given me explicit instructions on how to have fun, but I had done nothing they had recommended. Danny Bowden, a friend I met at the Alexandria church, tried his best to pull a good time out of me. He lost to Kennedy's campaign and to the voices from back home that were calling me to some form of social action. But maybe now was the time to have fun, since it appeared as if my forays into the domestic offensive were over.

With so little time left, maybe I would live up to my own plans of being a soldier like Ma Ponk's boys, Melvin and Sidney, during World War II. As a little boy, I had discovered a stash of exotic photographs hidden in Ma Ponk's black patent leather purse. I found them by accident as I rummaged through what we called the "shiftfro," the chest of drawers where my old aunt kept her good clothes, good jewelry, letters from her boys, her medicine, and cans of Garrett Snuff with the labels removed. I was just searching for something to amuse me when the purse fell out and with it pictures of pretty women with my handsome cousins all dressed in their uniforms and looking good. Those faded pictures, which were the closest things to sensual photographs I had ever seen, fueled my imagination and fantasy. I was going to sneak away from Ma Ponk's watchful eye to become a man in St. Louis. I tried. But just as I was deflected from real adventure by Marguerite in Washington, I was headed off in St. Louis.

Never having "slow-dragged" at the joints back home— where the smell of frying lard mingled mysteriously with the scent of Old Spice cologne and Lucky Heart perfume—I had looked forward to the freedom to experience the night life of Gas Light Square in St. Louis. However, soon after I arrived, I started attending Lively Stone's Church. The pastor was Elder Scott, whose rules of conduct were even more stringent than Ma Ponk's. A few of my friends from the youth group at church tried to sneak into the world where Afros were commonplace, smoke of all kinds filled the air, and Marvin Gaye's voice set the tone. But Elder Scott dared us to enjoy such entertainments.

Now I was approaching my last chance to leave the service with a late-night memory. Sgt. Myrick and his friends had been trying to get me to loosen up a bit, go out and have some fun, but I had politely turned their offers down, devoting all my extra time to school and political volunteering. This was the time to take them up on their offer. I needed to do something to snap me out of my depression. Those faded pictures at Ma Ponk's and old *Esquire* magazines that Aunt Willie Mae brought me from the houses where she worked had entertained me when I was boy; surely a real date with a real woman couldn't hurt.

Sgt. Myrick and his friends had already concluded that I was never going to be wild, so they worked on trying to fix me up with Gloria, a college girl from Howard University. They had it all planned. All I had to do was say "yes," which I surprised them at last by doing. According to them, Gloria and I were perfect for each other, and they arranged it all. They gave me her name and phone number and told her to expect my call. When I hesitated, they pushed. One of the airmen on base lent me his car. To go to class in College Park, I often had to hitchhike, but for this date, I was being given a car. I couldn't believe it. I couldn't even drive, at least not with the surety one needed in the city. I had learned to drive on the gravel road near the corner house owned by a lady we called simply Miss Big Dump. On the road by her house, you'd never encounter a traffic jam or a street light. In fact, it if had not been for the public water hydrant, I would have had nothing to hit. My stepfather went through great agony when I was sixteen and he let me drive his 1957 Chevy, whose gears I stripped for twenty-eight miles on the way to Greenville on my first real date, with Delores Braxton.

That was not a story I would tell the guys. I would just accept the keys and pray that the expressway would be empty and I could find my way around the one-way streets. I couldn't afford an accident. When I finally stopped worrying about the car and called Gloria, she seemed nice, and we quickly made a date. I had never dated a college woman before, and this one was almost through college, with plans to get her master's.

When the date night finally came, I dressed twice. I had to look my best. I wanted to appear cool. Driving a borrowed car didn't help. I managed the Beltway, but the big challenge, Georgia Avenue, lay ahead. "Why this street, of all places, a street hidden behind circles and one-way streets," I fumed. In spite of all my efforts to be prompt, I got there late, couldn't find a place to park, and had to run three long blocks to Gloria's dorm. I started to turn around at least twenty times, but the need for fun pushed me on. I threaded my way through construction that blocked nearly every sidewalk. As I kept looking for her dorm, I tried desperately to picture the evening. Would she really like going out with a soldier? Was she being teased and advised to watch out?

Would she be a dove or a hawk? Being black, she would likely be somewhat against the war and concerned about civil rights. I couldn't pretend that I had ever marched, chanted, or participated in a sit-in, but I had worked in Kennedy's campaign, and I knew that would count for something. I also knew Spike Ayers, the activist from Glen Allan. And of course, I could talk about my sister being jailed at Ole Miss.

The dorm looked sort of like a two-story barracks, but young men and women stood around the entry, and as the doors opened and shut, I could hear a lot of laughter. I watched for a moment or two as young men and young women moved in and out of the lobby. The more I saw of them, the more uncomfortable and military I felt. We were the same color, but they seemed to be speaking a different language, a confident college one.

I hesitated before I finally walked into the lobby, which was alive with college women and men visiting or leaving on their dates. They were all in their own world. No one seemed bothered by me but me. As I checked out the women, I wondered if I was going to be lucky. Most guys are never quite comfortable with blind dates. We seem to forget that on the other side, the date is also dealing with her questions. Who is this man who can't get a date on his own? As I stood there, I suddenly realized that Gloria had asked me to call her room when I arrived. I quickly found a phone, and when I heard her say "I'll be right down," my heart, which should have been light, sank to the floor. This was my first blind date ever, and at Howard University, one of the crown jewels of black colleges, where the best and the brightest went to school. Here I was, a soldier, trying to go out with a Howard woman, and not a clue about how to act.

"Clifton?" I heard my name and turned around. "Gloria?" There she was, a slender, attractive girl who smiled with an air of liberated college confidence as she walked toward me. As she drew closer, I wondered, "What does she think of me?" When she reached out her hand, I noticed her hair, her black dress, and her slim body. We chatted briefly and joined the other couples headed out into the night.

We found the car more quickly than I had thought and drove to a movie that was a safe choice for a first date. Over the course of the evening we talked a lot. We held hands. I was nervous. She was nice. I learned from her that the Southern Christian Leadership Conference, now led by Rev. Abernathy, had decided to proceed with the Poor People's Campaign in spite of Dr. King's death and the assassination of Robert Kennedy. I was elated. I could go back into the "fields." She may have thought that it was her attractiveness and conversational skills that excited me, but it was much more than that. Here would be one more chance to participate in history.

The decision to camp out in the nation's capital had a special significance for me. I had never marched in the movement. I had never run from a growling dog. Water hoses at full force had never been turned on me. My life had not been in danger, not once. I wanted to be part of the second great Washington assembly. Dr. King had been last on the program in 1963. His unprepared text, which came from a prepared heart, had caught and held our attention. I didn't know if this gathering would do for the nation what the former one had done, but I was close enough to find out for myself.

The media and the planners were projecting hundreds of thousands, perhaps a repeat performance. The call for "the poor" had gone out all over America, and they and their supporters were expected to come and, with their presence, dramatize the disparity between those who sat at America's table of plenty and the rest of the family, who only managed to live in the table's shadow. With Dr. King no longer alive to draw the crowds, the planners talked about the line-up of entertainers who were scheduled to lend their names and presence.

I wanted to see the stars, but I wanted to walk on the tracks of history even more. Although deep down I was unsure of the value of parading "the poor" before the world, I made my plans to be there. I fully expected to see people I knew from Glen Allan and suddenly wondered if they would come as civil rights workers or as poor people. I had never thought of them as "poor," but maybe they were, and maybe I had been. If we were, we never knew it. There was no stigma attached to living in shotgun houses, maybe because there were so many; and I thought every home had a rollaway bed stored behind the washing machine. A new stratum of folk was now being officially defined. Where would my people be? If income became the measure, many of the people I had known all my life were poor. And if they were coming, I wanted to be there.

Just as Ma Ponk had told me, the white boys with pony tails and cameras slung over their backs were there to give us a minute-by-minute, day-by-day account of the fifteen-acre stretch of green slowly becoming a field of portable toilets and marked-out dwelling spaces. Rev. Abernathy was there extolling the crowds and welcoming the "poor." The event was shaping up in spite of the voices that spoke against it. It was also becoming a place where both the curious and the caring with hand-held cameras walked the perimeters of the camp, taking the pictures that captured history. As I watched the news and made plans to be there on the weekend, the gathering place appeared to be losing the somberness of its purpose, becoming to me more like a big top where the curiosity seekers were coming to see the rare and unusual, not kith and kin. I knew better; these people were not sideshow oddities but Americans upon many of whose backs the nation had been built.

Wally, my dependable friend, gave me a ride into the District. For as long as possible I wanted to absorb the total feel of the life that was now set down between the Lincoln Memorial and Washington Monument. The day was hot and sticky, just like a Delta day. Except for the massive buildings and federal sites, the area looked like an overcrowded Delta. Thousands of people walked toward and around what had now begun to be called Resurrection City. As I walked among the curious and the caring, I tried to feel the electricity of involvement. I had come to have my batteries recharged, to rekindle the feeling I had enjoyed in 1963, when I watched on TV the great gathering at the Lincoln Memorial. I walked and looked. I listened and observed. Instead of feeling a great emotional surge, I felt only the loneliness of the people I saw. Many, straight from small towns, seemed lost in this makeshift city surrounded by people like us who had come to watch.

Here, among the public monuments of marble and stone, they took shelter in old canvas tents, hollowed-out buses, and the backs of trucks. As I watched the adults and the innocence of their children, I wanted to do something. I felt something. Not the spark of emotional excitement I had come looking to find, but hurt and pain. It was clear to me that these people had never been and might never be seated at the table of plenty. Where was the table? And would they ever find a place? Their plight was different from that of racism, an enemy that was not too difficult to spot or define. The problem here lay deeper than not being permitted to vote. The legal barrier to that challenge was known. No, this ancient human problem was called "poverty," and we were being challenged to do something about it. The masses of people, the ones we were calling "the poor," were present, but others spoke for them and the entertainers sang to them. I was glad I was there but uncomfortable as well. I wondered if, in this grand attempt to expose their need to the nation, their dignity had been left intact.

As I looked upon the crowd, I knew I could call out a

name like Mattie, "little bit," Buddy, or Shug, and some-body would answer. At moments I thought I recognized faces, faces that stopped and stared at me. I had seen similar faces many times back home. We had picked and chopped cotton together. We had ridden in the back of Mr. Walter's field truck, and we had gone to church together. I knew some of the eyes from Franklin Street in St. Louis and from the projects in Chicago. As I slowly circled their world, I saw their children shielded by their innocence, just standing, watching, and being children.

I left feeling powerless, not sure of what I could do or what the thousands of people I had seen really wanted us to do. Back home, the folk I knew just wanted all the bar-riers down that had relegated them to a lower social status and had also, in many cases, imposed on them a lack of material goods. Though they lived in small homes with few conveniences and ate a simple diet, I had also shared in the richness of their faith, their nurturing world, and their unselfish ability to see their future through the lengthening steps of their children. I had no sense of those possibilities and comforts for the people gathered here. There were many speeches, none that I remember. No single dream was shared, and I felt powerless to change the "City of the Poor" into the suburbs of plenty. I couldn't change them, but what I saw would continue to change me. It was get-ting close to the end of my season in the military, and I had witnessed a moment in history that I would continue to ponder for years to come.

EIGHT

Journeying On

As *August 18 drew near*, my long journey north from my small room in Ma Ponk's house was just about to end. Some of what I had feared had never happened. Shaped and fashioned by the world I encountered, I was no longer a young colored boy riding in a train filled with strangers. I had become a man during one of America's most difficult periods of growth, a time when new traditions were being established and new alliances formed, and when the innocence of a people and a nation had seemed to melt away.

In a few short months, I would be leaving the world of

the Eighty-ninth Presidential Wing to the capable hands of T.Sgt. Williams and Sgt. Myrick, both of whom were career airmen. They would continue to be polished and prepared, looking to initiate the new man who would take my place. Many of my friends outside of the military, those from the King Street Assembly and those I met while working on Robert Kennedy's campaign, would remain in the world surrounded by the Washington-Maryland Beltway.

Although encouraged to reenlist, I had just about decided that getting out was the right choice for me. Since my first permanent assignment at Dow Air Force Base, I had taken college courses every chance I got, and in a few days I would go down to the Base Education Office to make sure my transcripts were in order. No matter how rational the argument for reenlisting had become, I was determined to make my own decision.

During my last days at the Eighty-ninth, my leaving became the Monday morning talk. As soon as I came into work, the others would converge around my gray metal desk. Sgt. Myrick and T.Sgt. Williams, both neatly dressed and always sipping steaming cups of hot coffee, took turns pointing out why I should stay. Sgt. Myrick argued for all the advantages that I would have because of the Eighty-ninth Wing and the ease of completing college on the University of Maryland campus. Of course I heard what he didn't say as well: that I was black and so was he, and race appeared not to have stalled his military career. He seemed pleased with what he had accomplished and confident that I, too, could do well.

T.Sgt. Williams also argued persuasively. The military had been good to him, and he wore his enlistment with pride. He was without question an inside man. He knew the ropes, although he never shared the shortcuts he had learned. A career man, he had come in young, had steadily advanced, had gone to college, and would come out with the prospect of working for his U.S. Senator, Birch Bayh.

Myrick and Williams also argued that the outside world, especially the major cities, were continuing to be sites of violence and riots. And I remembered how hard and disappointing it had been at first for me as a black man to get a good job in St. Louis, the city of my dreams. That disappointment had for the first time brought me face to face with the reality of the North, shaking my boyhood dreams. Nevertheless, I did have one concrete objective in mind—completing college—and I wasn't afraid to face uncertainty beyond that point.

My military training had not crystallized a career in my mind, but I knew I would go to college. In fact, I had no other choice. It was a promise I had made to Poppa, now deceased, and I had to live up to my word. My civilian friends in Washington, several of whom were influential, wanted me to stay and go to Howard or Georgetown. One of the most insistent was the wife of Warren Rogers, then the editor of *Look* magazine, who said that since I was bright I had a responsibility to prepare for my future in the best possible educational environment. I was hesitant. Although I enjoyed the city, I found it complicated. And the prospect of looking for a place to live, getting a car to drive, and in general negotiating city life was almost like another enlistment. I needed some space and a way to ease into civilian life. Even with the carrot of a dependable retirement check dangling in front of me and T.Sgt. Williams's subtle hints, I didn't think I would stay.

More than my future was at stake. I had to honor the dreams of all the family and friends who had taken the time to set my sights beyond the cotton fields of the Delta. I had headed north to do well for all of us. My life had been temporarily interrupted by a war, for which they would excuse me; but I knew I would hear their voices challenging me not to take the easy road, and not to let our shared dreams fall apart. They knew the value of striking out to find the future that starts within your heart. It was that conviction that had undergirded their survival. Their voices were clear. I had to amount to something.

Each day of my life they knew that I would awaken with the skin color that many would use to define what I could or could not do. But my elders knew my worth. From their front porches, they had set out to create a world of protection and invitation where they nourished our roots. Knowing that we were growing up in a world where some folks would define us in belittling ways, they took it upon themselves to give us a truer picture of ourselves, where we came from, and what we had the potential to become. For them the military and doing well up north were steps along the road. I knew what they meant. The military had begun to recognize what they already knew, which would later be reflected in the broader society. They expected me to succeed in the service, go to college, and make them proud as I followed my heart into the future. They didn't want me to get out and drop out, as my Uncle Eugene had done. They expected more from me, just as they had expected more from Eugene. Thinking about what happened to him was scary. We had all believed in him.

My uncle had gone into the service, but after he was discharged, he lost his vision and disappointed everybody's dreams. He was expected to carry the family's torch into the future. He had graduated from O'Bannon High School a few years ahead of me, and with great family fanfare he went off to the military. His Aunt Mattie was excited. She had raised him after his mother, Miss Nola, died. He had been a bit feisty in school, and Mattie had had to go see the principal a few times, but his leaving, going off to better himself, had made her proud. With Eugene in uniform and sending back money each month, she could walk uptown, hold her head high, and pray for the best. When she went to the post office to pick up the small packages that Eugene sent home, they always contained a silk pillow. Miss Mattie proudly placed these pillows and the Asian animal carvings he had sent all around her front room.

Eugene was in the service, and that was honorable. The

pillows were there to show all the people. His uniformed picture was placed beside a portrait of his mother that she had sent home years before during a short stay in St. Louis. Eugene's picture was turned in such a way that you'd see it the minute you walked in. Miss Mattie was proud of Gene, as she called him, and rightly so. Her generation, as had that of Poppa Young and Ma Ponk, expected their children to achieve, do better than they themselves had done, set a good example, and bring others along.

Eugene had access to the nurturing community, and Miss Mattie had always wanted the best for him. There was no reason not to expect his enlistment to be a stepping stone to bigger and better things. We all enjoyed his enlistment and expected great things of him when he returned. Would he go straight to college? Or would he go up north and stay for a while with his father's family? No one was sure, but we all were excited. Our Gene had gone off to do good.

After his enlistment was up, he came back as we all expected. He looked good. He spoke with more polish than he had before, and he gave us money. On the first few days, he wore his army uniform as he strolled about town. The old folk talked with him from their front porches. The old men even made a place for him at the card tables. And as the younger nephew tagging along, I heard the deep, mature laughter from the men as he pulled out pictures of the exotic women he had met. This went on for a week or two, and then I began to notice that no one except Gene was laughing much anymore.

He had been at home long enough to talk about what he was going to make of himself, but he had not mentioned any plans. And they all knew he couldn't just play checkers with them for the rest of his life. So they began slowly not to have room for him. They were excited about his return but troubled at his seeming to stay at home too long. Later I would come to understand that as he sat too long in their midst just drinking, laughing, and telling the same old jokes, they didn't see any realization of the future they had woven into him. They had bet on him, but somehow he never moved ahead. The uniform had done him little good, and the disappointment could be seen in their eyes. We had both passed the same porches, but I had stopped and listened. We had both seen the old people, but I had taken the time to hear their voices and to know their hearts, as had many of the other youth. Poppa and Ma Ponk had caught my attention early and had impressed upon me the responsibility I had to them and the family who had gone before me.

Now, as I prepared to reenter civilian life, I understood even more why both Sgt. Myrick and T.Sgt. Williams wanted me to be sure that I had thought through all my options and had given due consideration to remaining in the service and continuing college. I realized the challenge that lay ahead, and I valued their concerns. I had a future, though, that was grounded in the solid dreams of people who would not give up. Back home in Glen Allan, as well as in St. Louis, there were people to whom I felt accountable, and, no matter where I was, I would finish college.

Poppa and Mama Pearl had set the standards. They ignored the restrictions of legal segregation and dreamed of college for my mother, Mary. She started but never quite finished. I had to finish. I was the oldest child, and for my family I was the lead man. I refused to let my mind dwell on the fact that I had signed a document at Jefferson Bank and Trust in St. Louis that would have provided employment for me when I completed my enlistment. I had no plans to go back to St. Louis. It was the right place in June of 1963. For my future, I needed a new fertile field. College would be that field.

I was keenly aware that life on college campuses, now was not quite as I had remembered from my visits to Alcorn as a child. On many traditional campuses the voices of Black Muslims were now being heard. Many of us had been motivated by the nonviolence and inclusive teachings of Dr. Martin Luther King, but now, the persistence of racism brought the voices of Elijah Mohammed and Malcolm X into our lives. And in college, I would probably have to confront still other militant voices. Where would I fit in? I had been a student-in-waiting while some of them had been workers in the fields. I had lived a premilitary life of separate but equal, whereas they had already challenged both the morality and constitutionality of such a lifestyle. While I had been learning to become a sharpshooter, many of them had become Freedom Riders going back to my South to put into the hands of my people a weapon more powerful than the gun, the right to vote.

And who had I become? What were my goals? After getting my discharge, carefully folding my air force blues, and putting my official discharge papers away, who would I be? As my decision time got closer, I could almost hear Poppa's voice humming that tune reminding me that to worry was to waste time. I had to run with what I had because I could not hold time in my hands.

Soon I would be a veteran. The uniform that I had learned to wear with distinction and pride was perceived by some, on college campuses especially, as a cloak of subversive capitalism, certainly not a garment one would wear after it was no longer required. I didn't feel that way. I didn't own a major company. I had no subversive plans. I had earned the right to wear the uniform, even though the war it may have represented was questionable to many, even myself. The uniform had always been revered back home, and soldiers were always welcomed back to tell their tales of life beyond the oceans. Their stories had once fueled many dreams about the prospects of a new, different, and better life for the Negro in America. Unlike World War II or even the Korean war, Vietnam was a war that nobody claimed, and it spawned no dreams.

After listening to all of my officers and friends, I knew

that another reason I could not take their advice was that I felt a pull to Oklahoma, which had taken hold when I was a youngster. Even though I had by now traveled further than I had ever dreamed and had glimpsed a world that drew me beyond the segregated world of my childhood, I had not forgotten an important letter that I had received when I was in high school. In those days, some of my classmates and I were looking for enlightened colleges that would open their doors to bright young colored boys and girls. We wanted to attend such schools alongside whites to help dispel the myth of so-called white superiority. During that time, I made application to the newly started Oral Roberts University in Tulsa, about which I had heard good things. Yet I was still apprehensive about whether or not they would accept colored students. To ease my fears, I sat down one day and wrote a very pointed letter to the university asking if my race would stand in the way. When Chuck Ramsey, dean of admissions at ORU, wrote to assure me that I would be welcome there, I took his letter as evidence of the integration I had dreamed about but had not seen. And throughout my time in St. Louis and the military, I always kept his letter with me. I knew that outside the military the fight for integration was still a matter of fierce struggle and debate. However, my well-worn letter from Mr. Ramsey certified for me that there was indeed a place where I could find the integrated America I had sought as a child and still believed in.

I knew the school and its founder to be controversial. I

didn't care. In a place where integration was embraced as an ideal, I would fulfill my childhood dream of completing college. And I was pretty sure I wouldn't be bothered by the religious focus of the place. After all, I had been reared in the midst of Baptist preachers and deacons. Although I had learned a lot in the military, it had been a detour. Going to Oral Roberts University would put me back on the road I had hoped to travel before the detour occurred. I felt that I would be in charge again and could pursue a life of my own choosing.

By now, it had become clear to my military friends that I would not reenlist. They all knew that I had decided to head west to Oklahoma—a place Mama Pearl had called "way out yonder" years before, when my Poppa went there by train to attend a black Baptist convention. All that was left was a series of planned debriefings, which I had to go through as a member of the classified Eighty-ninth. As the debriefings came to an end, and I was asked to swear that I would not talk about my job, I was also given a last-minute chance to reenlist. But I had made up my mind.

Nevertheless, I still searched for a single sign, one that would provide me the same kind of confidence I had felt years earlier when I decided to leave home. After August 18, I would be on my own. There would be no military code of justice to direct and control my actions. I would be a civilian in America with the freedom to become involved in the movements still going on, to voice my opinions about the war, and perhaps to go south and enlist in the struggle that was still very much alive. In this new life, I could criticize and be criticized. I would now be measured by my own actions, efforts, and determination.

This had been the case when I was a youngster picking cotton. The value of that last sack of cotton, in those last hours of the day, would determine whether our entire day was a winner. Now, these old feelings of last-hour challenge were surfacing. Just as back then, knots were in my stomach as I was faced with my new challenge. I had to make the right choice or else my previous efforts would be lost.

While contemplating my decision, I marked time off the calendar, just as we had watched the sun and marked off the hours in the cotton fields. The seasoned eyes of the old field workers had watched the sun and bid us to hurry. We had to pick fast and hope that when we weighed the cotton we would find we had set ourselves a new picking record, one that would make us proud tomorrow.

Off in the distance, we could see the caretakers of that future—the trailer, the iron scales, and Mr. Walter, with his ever-present toothpick in his mouth, just waiting to answer our fear or reward our faith. The end road filled as the sun dipped further west and the fields emptied of all the friends, uncles, aunts, and cousins who labored there. Laughter, yells, and some disappointed slaps would meld together as those last sacks of cotton were brought up to Mr. Walter to be weighed. Some felt cheated and told him so, while others just added up the numbers of all their efforts and, with their last sack weighed and numbers right, gave a happy shout.

That same kind of confidence was building as I settled my last decision. After four years in the service, during a war that seemed to have no end and with the struggle for equality still making the front pages, I would return to civilian life and resume the journey of making my elders proud of me, of becoming somebody for them. During my years in the military, much that my people had planted was ready for harvest, and the crops were coming in. Although I had been more of an observer than a participant, I was nonetheless able to set my feet on an honest path because the voices of the porch people who were with me as a boy never left when I became a man. The memory of their love continued to nurture and sustain me and would accompany me as I again packed my belongings and, with airline tickets in hand, made ready to fly west to Oklahoma.

It had all started so many years ago, when I was just a young colored boy growing up in the Mississippi Delta with dreams of going north.

EPILOGUE

Old Fields Visited

Of all the things I learned during the 1960s, none was more striking than the discovery that the North was not the promised land. Leaving home as a boy, I had gladly anticipated the changes of habit and fortune that my northern relatives had pictured for us on their visits home, but I was totally unprepared for the changes that I found. In St. Louis, where I had gone to experience my version of the North, I watched as William Clay led city youth into the streets—not to be baptized in an urban version of Lake Washington back home, but to demand their rights, rights that I had already thought were theirs. And instead of the grand life I had heard of when "Chicago" and "Detroit" would come south to visit, I came to see a different North, an often incendiary place that made no promises and offered no real comfort to the soul. Instead, it was the South that I returned home to visit in 1967 that showed me great strength and hope in the struggle.

For me, no one was more prominent in that struggle than Spike Ayers, who continued to fight for years not only for our town but for proper funding for the black colleges in our home state. Along with his contribution to the civil rights struggle, Spike will be remembered as the initiator of the 1972 *Ayers* v. *Fordice* lawsuit, the most significant case on the quality and accessibility of education for African Americans since *Brown* v. *Board of Education* in 1954. The case came into being when Spike began helping a group of parents and students who alleged that the state of Mississippi had maintained racial segregation by perpetuating a dual system of postsecondary education. Though initiated to simply require the state to adopt and implement a policy of equity in the funding of higher education, the case has caused the courts to look at Mississippi's entire public college and university system, resulting in the controversial review of the costly duel programiming with the potential for college closings and mergings.

Spike Ayers died of a heart attack in 1986, at age sixty-six. It pleases me no end that he survived all the external perils that he faced, that he was from Glen Allan, my hometown, and that I saw him becoming a leader during the harvest years of the 1960s.

The South's significance as the site of struggle and hope was underscored for me in 1993, when I received an invitation from Nancy Anderson, an English professor at Auburn University at Montgomery, to lecture at the Auburn University Fall Book Harvest later in the year. I had never been to Montgomery, although I had heard about it most of my life. It was there that Rosa Parks essentially started the civil rights movement by refusing to move to the back of the bus. And it was there that a young preacher, Dr. Martin Luther King Jr., caught the eye of the media as he began organizing for justice and speaking out.

Years before, on the six o'clock news, I had glimpsed a new America in the tense, expectant faces of men and women of all races who gathered in Montgomery, joined hands, and defied the social order of the day. And it was there, in their repeated singing of "We Shall Overcome," that a national anthem for the movement was born. As the world watched, Montgomery became more than a southern city whose roots were deep in slavery—it became a shrine, a place where major civil rights offensives had their start.

Even though my invitation to speak in Montgomery came some twenty-seven years later, I was elated to be going to the city that, in my mind, summed up the struggle. I wanted to see, feel, and touch the relics of the movement and incorporate their meaning into my life. During the sixties, when I was a teenager and then a soldier, young people my age had sought justice by nonviolent means, and some had been killed and wounded along the way. As I thought about my visit, I could still hear the name calling they had endured—yells of "nigger" and "nigger lover" that went right to your bones—but I could also see the calm, bespectacled face of Rosa Parks as she held her seat on the bus and hear the galvanizing words of Dr. Martin Luther King Jr.: "We, the citizens of Montgomery . . ."

My Montgomery hosts, Craig and Betsy Sheldon, were to meet me at the airport. They had read my first book, *When We Were Colored*, and volunteered to host me for the weekend, and I had already received a warm letter from them. Almost three decades after the movement, white people would welcome me to a city where years earlier other whites had cried "Nigger, go home" to other blacks.

My book, our only common bond, allowed the three of us to reflect on our experiences as southerners. The more we talked, the more we realized that our worlds had been maturing at about the same time. There was one special difference: Craig had come of age in the city where the modern civil rights movement began, and what I had watched from a distance, he had witnessed firsthand. He had been one of the "good" white people Poppa had spoken of. He had anguished with us and shared the belief that all people truly were created equal.

Whiskered, slightly balding, and with an emotional voice, he and his wife, a transplanted Easterner, volunteered to walk back in time with me. Our first stop after a drive down a quiet southern boulevard was the Alabama capitol building, which I had seen on television many times. Here it was, with its imposing white facade. Surrounded by military statues, it sat silently in the sun. We parked nearby, and as my hosts slowly walked me from the capitol to the Dexter Avenue Baptist Church, where Dr. King had served, I could not believe that Governor George Wallace's office had sat so close to Dr. King's. So far apart were the two men politically that I had assumed they had had offices on opposite sides of town. With a good arm, Governor Wallace could easily have tossed a football into the waiting arms of Dr. King as he stood on the steps of the church.

I felt little need to talk. As we passed places where police officers not unlike the infamous Birmingham sheriff, T. Bull Conner, stood and ordered actions that had caused hearts to tremble, I silently tried to imagine the furious voices who had struggled to hold history in check.

It appeared to be an unusually quiet day in Montgomery. Except for the three of us, I saw few people walking. When it was almost time to go back to the car, the Sheldons suggested that we walk one block further, to the Southern Poverty Law Center, so I could see the civil rights memorial there. As we crossed the street to the center, I stopped to let an elderly black man pass. He was the first black person I had seen. He was pushing an old bicycle to which were strapped cooking utensils, a blanket, clothes—an odd assortment of things. A homeless man, I thought. Poorly dressed and in dire need of a shave, he quickly looked away when I caught his eye and hurried off, pushing his old bike. He was in his own world, like a man from another time, but in the moment that our eyes met, I knew I saw my brother. I said nothing to my hosts, who had walked on ahead of me, but seeing this old man with his bike still searching for a place to call home made me realize how far we had to go to make "America" a reality for us all. At the same time, I looked up at the Sheldons, who were waiting for me to catch up with them, and realized how far we had come as a people.

At the center, other visitors stood silently before a large, flat, circular marble stone that looked like an ancient timepiece. It was designed so that cool, clear water would always caress the names of the martyred and slain—Evers, King, Schwerner, Cheney, Goodman, Liuzzo. . . . Tears sprang to my eyes. These people had stood, lived, and died in my stead.

I was glad when Craig checked his watch and suggested that they get me to the hotel so that I could dress for my lecture that night. On the way, I learned that we had an acquaintance in common, attorney Delores Boyd, who had

gone to college with me in Oklahoma and had now distinguished herself as a black, female, southern lawyer, and
that I would get to see her.

The next afternoon, they took me to Delores's bookstore, Roots and Wings. After we chatted for a while about
old times, Delores offered to take me to see other places in
Montgomery that were sacred to the movement. Our first
stop was the bus stop Rosa Parks had used. We parked
nearby and got out to look around. To passing motorists, it
probably looked as if two black people were just out shop-
ping and had paused to chat. But as I stood there in front
of a closed movie house with faded posters peeling from its
walls and an empty lot where scattered clumps of Johnson
grass pushed up through the concrete, my heart swelled
with a sense of the significance of this place. I touched a
cold gray parking meter on which Rosa Parks could have
rested her tired hands on her way to the bus stop, just a
few feet away.

It was quiet again today, but in my mind, I heard the
rumble of a bus and envisioned Rosa Parks and others
boarding it, unaware that history would be made. I could
almost imagine stepping onto the bus with them and the
looks on the faces of those who watched Mrs. Parks defy
the order of the day. But I quickly returned to reality as I
heard an actual Montgomery city bus move slowly up the
street. The same bus? Couldn't be. Today, I had no need to
flag it down. It didn't stop as Rosa Parks's bus had done
nearly thirty years before. It just passed us by, slowly

moving toward a future of its own. The prominent role of the bus moving our lives had obviously changed.

I was moved by Delores's commitment to her people and the restoration of her South. Driving fast, pointing, and talking all at once, she navigated the streets of Montgomery with ease. As she approached the old bus station on South Court Street, once a busy port of entry and departure, her voice grew sad. This was the place, she said, that the Freedom Riders had been beaten. "I was just a girl, but I'll always remember the night it happened. The older people had been told to expect trouble, so they kept us locked in Reverend Ralph Abernathy's church—the First Baptist Church on Ripley Street. And trouble did come— which, though I was young, I'll never forget." The Freedom Riders, she said, had come to Montgomery to be trained to provide help in Mississippi. I had heard about the beatings when I was up north, but I had no idea that the people beaten had been on their way to the Delta.

Delores continued to point out places where as a child she had walked and lived. Where I saw superhighways, she said the land had once been home to thriving colored communities. Again, her voice grew sad. As we drove past a former Catholic hospital, she told me how it was one of the few places where the famous and not so famous came to start the marches that helped put Montgomery on the map.

We finished the tour at Delores's bookstore, where the Sheldons were waiting for me. It was an emotional day and a pilgrimage that I, as a black southerner, felt compelled to make. Montgomery, after all, was significant to many, perhaps especially to the people of Glen Allan. Many of those who had worked with Spike Ayers to bring equality to our town had been trained and challenged here, summoned by Montgomery's message, "Now is the time," which rang in the sixties throughout the South. Now I had seen this hallowed city for myself. I would no longer have to rely on pictures taken by strangers for my vision of the place. Delores Boyd and the Sheldons had helped me see it for myself, enriching my vision with their own, and I recalled once again how the civil rights movement changed my view of the world during the years when I watched the crops come in.

There was indeed no promised land. It was enough to have this land, this journey, this life.